From King of Karachi to Lockdown in the Costa del Crime: Meet the International Smuggler Who Dominated Europe's Worst Prison

By Chet Sandhu

ISBN:
ISBN-13: 978-1530593767
ISBN-10: 153059376X

Everyone left me when I was in jail. I know for a fact the people I asked for help were thinking: don't involve me in this. Out of all the gangsters and killers that I've been with, given the choice of one person to stand by me, I choose my Ma. She puts all the others to shame.

CONTENTS

1 JET KHAN

This is a story I never wanted to write down. It started from messages between me and friends on my Facebook page. As things turned out they liked my stories and encouraged me to write more, so I did. This book will offend some people, those I know and others who I have never met. I'm not bothered. This is my story and if anyone has a problem with it they should come and see me. I'm not hard to find. You also need to know that as you read these pages you're not going to learn about how I survived one of the most extreme prisons on the planet. Instead, you'll know how I came to dominate the hellhole I was thrown into.

I was pulled into the world of crime while I was living in Newcastle in the north of England. I'm from an immigrant Indian family, my father was a strict man, and he wanted me to grow up the traditional way. However, I was living in modern Britain and I wanted to embrace the opportunities I saw in front of me. For the young Chet Sandhu that meant money, girls, drugs, music, clothes in that order. I had to rebel. By my eighteenth year, I had been involved in a few fights, caused by my instinct to stick up for myself against other local lads. The police got involved, so my father told me to move out of the family home. As far as I was concerned, this was fair enough. I have always stayed in shape, people still see me as a big brown guy with a shaved head, tattoos and plenty of attitude. To survive on my own and give me the lifestyle I craved, I worked as a doorman in nightclubs. It was the 90's and the Ibiza club and drug scene had taken the UK by storm. By the time I hit my twenties I was well into body building and I had a good idea of the steroid market. There was a strong demand for these muscle-enhancing drugs among the people I trained with, so I decided to fill the gap in the market. The profit I generated made my doorman salary look like pocket money. I soon graduated from dealing to bringing gear (drugs) into the UK from Spain, Turkey and Greece. The mark-up meant I was doubling my investment each time I made a trip, but my addiction to the trappings of the club scene was sucking all my cash away quicker than I was making it. I needed to make more.

I knew from my bodybuilding contacts that Pakistan was one of the cheapest places in the world to buy steroids. I told my parents I was going over there, but not what I was going over for. I just said "business". They begged me not to, as at the time India and Pakistan were on the brink of war. My father warned me if the Pakistanis found out that I was Indian they would kidnap me and hold me to ransom, maybe even kill me. Kidnap was especially rife in Karachi, Pakistan's largest city and the place I needed to go to buy the drugs. In a situation like this, I knew it was sensible to bring backup. I had two cousins, Veeru and Jai who were the obvious choice. We were all doormen at the time, and we felt we could handle ourselves. Jai was a bit older than me, he was big at six foot, two inches tall. Veeru was only about eighteen years old, but he was still six foot and well-built. We were earning about fifty pounds per-night on the door, which in my opinion was chicken feed. Through buying and selling steroids on the street in England, I was making about one thousand pounds per-week. Back in the nineties this was decent dollar, but I was hungry for more and I wasn't scared of taking the risks necessary to get more. The way I saw it the world was a big vagina and I wanted to stick my cock right in it and swirl it around. The three of us agreed to go over to Karachi, and each bring back a suitcase packed with steroids. We gave each other Muslim names, so we wouldn't raise concern from the Pakistanis. My name was Jet Khan.

We landed in Karachi at seven in the evening. We found ourselves in a busy and dirty city, similar to the ones I was knew about from visits to family back in India. I was excited about what was to come. We got into a taxi.

"Where's the party hotel?" I said to the driver. He replied by saying he didn't know what I was talking about. I persisted. "Hotel with girls." The driver just looked at me as if I was talking Japanese. I said to my two cousins. "Let's get another taxi."

We bailed that one and suddenly loads of drivers were coming to us to take us. "Hang back and let me sort this," I said. A small guy with a moustache came up and started talking in Punjabi to me, which is also spoken in the part of India my parents were from, so I replied like a native. I asked if he knew where the nearest brass house was. The term "brass" comes from Cockney Rhyming Slang. It is deciphered like this: brass nail-tail, "tail" = prostitute.

He said, "Sure. My name is Kosa," he went to shake my hand, so I took it. I liked his confident style. I knew immediately this was the guy that wouldn't fail me out there. Kosa took the three of us to the Paradise hotel in central Karachi. It was a concrete block, eight stories high, and at the very top we found the party floor. This is where prostitutes from Russia and Turkey stayed, so this was where we wanted to be. We got a room each.

There were about twenty rooms in total up on the eighth floor. Five of these rooms were for the brass, there were two in each room. The Russian girls were very popular, and the Turkish seemed very exotic to me as I had never seen a Turkish brass before. Once the three of us from England were settled, I summoned the porter. I told him to tell the girls that there were some new kids on the block. I made him understand we weren't shy about spending cash. "Send them all to my room to say hello," I said.

My man didn't let me down. Within five minutes eight girls walked through the door, led by the Madame. Out of the eight there were only three I would actually have shagged, but I thought that was not a bad ratio. We introduced ourselves and so did they. The girls seemed nervous, as we were all big whereas the Pakistani folk I saw were normally quite small. I remember one billboard I saw in Karachi said in English, "Make up for the smallness of your size - join the Pakistan army."

Our first meeting with gaggle of brass was a bit awkward, but they seemed to like us in a shy way as we weren't immediately sleazing on them, which was what normally happened out there. Once the girls left, Veeru immediately jumped up and said, "I want one of them."

There was a young fit girl from Turkey, and I knew this is the one Veeru had his eye on. You could see his eyes ignite when she walked in. So I said go for it. He said, "I don't know what to say to her." So I went to talk on his behalf.

I walked into their room and all eight girls and the Madam were sat there. They all started smiling when I walked in. I said, "I've come for my cousin 'cos he's shy."

The girls started laughing and speaking together in Russian. The Madame was about forty-years old and quite big, with mad eyebrows. She said to me, "Are you all going to be good boys?" I replied, "Sure," with a wink, thinking the Madame fancied me a bit.

I paid her two thousand rupees, which at the time was about forty British pounds. Girls weren't cheap in Pakistan. Prostitution was so underground, it was only for the wealthy. A forty quid session there was the same value as a weekly wage to the average person. I went back to Veeru's room and told him his bird would be landing soon. I decided we would party the rest of the night and get on with the job in hand tomorrow.

Jai, Kosa, and I went looking for alcohol. Kosa knew an underground place. In Karachi you couldn't buy alcohol in a normal shop like we were used to back home. Instead, Kosa brought us to a hut in a backstreet with a small barred window. The place looked dirty. I asked the bloke in the hut if he had any vodka and a bottle of Jack Daniels. He wanted to see my passport before he served me, so I showed it to him. He saw my real name and knew I was a British Indian. I pushed the dollar into his fist. He gave me a dirty look, but didn't say anything before giving the drink over. Back at the Paradise we partied all night. I got with one of the girls, her name was Sophia. She was 24 years-old and from Turkey. All the girls were drinking with us until about 5am, when the Madame came into my room. She ushered them all out and gave me a dirty look, presumably for getting her girls so wasted.

The next day we went looking for the factory that produced the type of steroids we were looking for, Sustanon. After hours of driving we eventually found it out in the sticks. I entered and spoke with the manager, Mr Ismail. He was a fat man in his late 40's with a brown suit on. I told him we wanted to buy 50,000 ampoules (each of these are the small sealed plastic vials steroids are contained in). Mr Ismail said it wasn't possible, as he was strictly regulated and only sold to pharmaceutical companies. I tried to bribe him, but my man wasn't having it. This was strange for Pakistan. The place was known for its widespread corruption. It was a day wasted. We would have to start again tomorrow.

We started doing the rounds at corner shop chemists. They had steroids, but only in very small amounts, which wouldn't do for our plans. After a few hours of this, I found out that there was a chemist that could get us the amount we wanted. I'm going to name them. I'll call them, Bang-on Traders. They had the steroid and pill market on lock down in Karachi. Nobody was allowed to sell in large amounts apart from them. I was hearing that they did a lot of business so we paid them a visit. These goons had shotguns under the counter, I was guessing because there was always a lot of money at Bang-on Traders. I spoke with the boss of the outfit. He was called Bashir. This guy was in his 40's and he looked like a religious Muslim with a beard but no tache. He even wore a prayer cap. Bashir was a big guy. We learned later that all the armed henchmen who surrounded him nearly all the time were in fact his sons. Bashir told me what he could supply me. He had everything: Rophenol, Diazepam, Temazepam, Temgesics the whole spectrum of legal drugs, anti-depressants and Viagra. They could also get a hold of any illegal drug I wanted, including heroin. This time, we just wanted Sustanon. Bashir was charging thirty pence per-amp, and I would sell in the UK for one pound forty pence in bulk. The value for a small vial sold on the streets of Newcastle was three pounds fifty pence. Bashir said he wanted payment immediately and the gear would turn up by the morning. We wanted 30,000 ampules of Sustanon, which was going to cost nine grand. This was a steal. At this rate we would make a minimum profit of thirty three thousand pounds from this one trip. Jai and Veernu didn't want to pay up front. But I trusted boss as he had a good set up. I said, "Ok" and gave him the money in a bag of notes. Bashir tapped on a hatch in the ceiling and this little kid appeared. The boss gave the boy our money and he scampered away.

We picked up the gear in the morning. There were a lot of boxes, so we got two taxis and took everything back to the Paradise Hotel. Then we would have to repack it all to get it into all our suitcases. Each ampule was in its own box and packaging. We had to take every amp out and then put six in each box to fit them all in. This was taking ages. I was getting blisters on my hands before we'd even done the first thousand. I complained to our driver, Kosa who promised he would sort it out. He started driving us about to see if he could find us a solution. I said I will pay him ten thousand rupees if he could manage it. At the time it was around forty rupees to-the-pound, so I was going to give him about two hundred and fifty quid. His wage at the time was 3,000 rupees per-week, so this bribe was a lot of money for him. Kosa was a good guy in his 30's. After just a few days he started to drink with us, so I trusted him. To keep him extra happy I also gave him two adult magazines, which you couldn't buy in Pakistan.

He was over the moon with joy. Kosa took all the gear and turned up the next day with it all packed down. It was all done perfectly and I was impressed. I asked how he got such a big task done so quickly. What he did was this. He gathered twenty young boys from the street into his house. Once he sat them all down together, Kosa showed them the cover of 'Men Only', the porn magazine I had given him. He slowly peeled back the cover and showed the youngsters the first page. The boys had never seen a naked white woman before, and they were clambering over each other to get a better look. They were going crazy. Kosa promised the boys they could see the next page if they pack one box of steroids. He had plenty of bargaining power because the mag was about forty pages long, but there were only twenty boxes of steroids. This is how he got the job done, and it didn't cost him a rupee.

2 THE CHIEF

We now had two-days left until the flight. We got drunk and partied right up until then. On the day, Veeru, Jai and me went into Karachi International Airport, and walked right up to the first set of security. The guards wanted our passports, which were British, but when they looked at our names and saw we were of Indian origin they told us to open up our suitcases, which we did. The guard's eyes bulged as they looked down to see all three cases packed full of steroids. We said we were bodybuilders, and insisted the tightly packed vials were for personal use. The group of guards just started laughing. Then they noticed a porn mag we had in the case. They started pointing at it in excitement.

I said, "Take the mag and here's another one. Just let us go." To my surprise one of them said, "Ok" and waved us on. We then went to the next stage, x-ray security. We had the same problem there, so again I offered one of the porn mags as a bribe. By this time we had two left - don't ask me why we bought so many. The x-ray guards took the mag gratefully. I couldn't believe we had bought off airport security with porn mags. It seemed like you could do anything in Pakistan if you had enough of them. We had a good drink on the flight, but once we changed at Amsterdam the journey became tense. We knew what was coming and that was Newcastle security. We hardly spoke to each other on this final leg. We got our bags from the conveyor belt and I headed up. I turned the corner to where British security officials were normally waiting, but nobody was there. I faced my two counterparts, Veeru and Jai, and smiled. It was all high fives in the airport car park. We sold the gear in a week, and made about ten thousand pounds each. We decided to go back to Pakistan within the month.

As soon as we got to Karachi we linked up with Kosa once again, and went to Bang-on-Traders. We bought the same amount as the last trip. But this time I bought some Valium as well, because there was also a good mark up on them. I told bossman Bashir about the problem of re-packaging. He said leave it to him.

"Everything will be here and packed in two days" he said. Bashir didn't even charge me for the re-packaging. We were left with a lot of time on our hands before our scheduled flight home, so we decided to have a look around Karachi. It had a few KFCs and Pizza Huts. The locals treated these like we treat bars, it was a big event to go there. One time during the day, the three of us were sat in a Pizza Hut. There were only about five other customers in the restaurant when about four shots were fired though the windows. We dived under the tables for cover, then it went silent. We had been caught in a drive-by shooting.

I said, "What the fuck?" to the staff. They explained shootings like this had happened a few times. There was a terrorist group that didn't like western restaurants being established in their hometown, so every now and then they go and shoot one of them up.

We were staying at our HQ, the top floor of the Hotel Paradise. The more nights we spent at the hotel, the more I got to know the girls who worked out of there, especially Sophia, who was pleased to see me again. We used to drink and have a laugh. One night I was in one of the rooms where all used to hang out, when three greasy-looking dudes turned up. One of them was the city's Chief of Police. In the room there were the three of us bodybuilding doorman from England, two girls, and now the three cops. The Chief introduced himself, and in turn I introduced myself as Jet Khan. We started drinking together, and during the course of the evening he asked why we were in Karachi.

"Family business," I said. The Urdu language he was speaking was similar to my native language, Punjabi. I could understand bits of it. Thinking I couldn't understand him, the Chief was talking to his mates.

"Jet looks like a Pakistani, but the other two don't." He turned and asked if I would I have sex with one of the girls in front of them? He was happy to pay. It sounded like a strange request, but I knew what was going down. Suspicious about our origins, these officers wanted to see if I was circumcised, which would reveal if I was a Muslim (which most Pakistanis are) or not. I decided to call his bluff.

"Yeah, ok," I replied. I had spent some time with the girl he fancied the most, and I knew she wouldn't take kindly to the offer of an orgy no matter what the price. If I came onto her strongly, I was sure she would be offended and refuse. So I did, and she said firmly, "No," to the Chief.

My two mates were getting nervous. They said they were tired and soon after went to bed. I stayed up drinking and smoking dope with the three cops. They seemed to like my style and took a shine to me. The Chief gave me his card, and said to call him if I got into any drama while we were in his city. He gave me a lump of hashish, and we said our goodbyes. I was paranoid this might be a setup, so I hid the hash in a plant pot a few rooms down the hall from us. But in the end nobody raided me.

The next day, Jai, Veeru and I were driving around with Kosa at about midnight, looking for a party. We were stopped by six military police on the back of an open jeep. These guys had a bad reputation, I had heard stories of them taking tourists into cells to extract money, or even kidnapping them and selling them to criminals and terrorists. The black-uniformed officers got out and began aggressively pointing their guns at us. Kosa was shit-scared.

"Don't fuck with them," he said. I got out the car, and said to the police, "Fuck you, I'm a British citizen you can't hold me." Kosa said just pay them off, but I'd had a drink so I wasn't having it.

I said, "This is my man," and I pulled out the Chief's business card, and told them to phone him and find out who I am. They went away to make their telephone call. The police came back, apologised and said we can go. My man the Chief had come out good.

3 IN THE VILLAGE

The next day my counterparts wanted to go scouting for females. Kosa said he knew a couple of girls in a village close by, so we decided to take a drive out there. Personally, I just went for the ride as I was quite happy with Sophia. We drove for about forty-five minutes, and ended up in a village in the middle of nowhere. With its wooden shelters, skinny-looking people, and simple donkey tracks, this place was totally different from the city. It felt like going back in time two-hundred years. We drove into the center of the settlement, and parked up. Kosa told us to wait where we were, to let him sort out the girls, and he left. In the meantime, we decided to stretch our legs.

Jai spotted a little shop. It was a hot day, so we decided to go get some fizzy drinks. While we were buying the pop, a couple of curious kids came over. They were only young. The three of us were all big and full of steroids at the time. The two boys smiled up at us, and one asked if we were wrestlers? We were the biggest people we ever saw in Karachi, and in this village we stood out even more than when we were in the big city. I said, "Yes, we are wrestlers." The kids got excited and ran away. Within half-a-minute, there were about thirty kids standing around us. I was showing off and giving them a double bicep pose. They were all getting excited. One of the kids said, "He's the Rock!" (in reference to the famous wrestler and actor, Dwayne Johnson). All the kids were jumping up and down, calling even more of their mates until there was a sea of little people all chanting after us. I have to admit the little people were very cute.

Kosa came back and said, "What the fuck? You've got no chance of going to the girl's house. The whole village is watching." Jai and Veernu were not happy, but this farce was their fault just as much as mine.

We told the kids we were going, but they were pulling at my vest and pants. I gave a few of them money, but this was a mistake. They were jumping on my back, slapping at my legs, and trying to wrestle me. We decided to make a break for the taxi, and the kids were running after us. Luckily we got in the car without any children attached to us, and Kosa sped off, leaving a cloud of dirt behind us. When I looked back from the car window, I saw the kids were still running and shouting after us. I turned round to my two mates and said, "Fuck. Now I know what Boyzone feel like."

Our flight was the next day, and we prepared our cases by packing the drug in tightly just like last time. Kosa dropped us off, wishing us a good flight with his toothless grin. We walked into the airport and went to the first set of security. It was the same lazy and greedy guards as last time, but now they wanted more than porn mags. We stood for ages, with these goons arguing about how much they wanted, and what we could give them.

After what seemed like hours we reluctantly paid them five-thousand rupees (about one-hundred and twenty-five pounds Sterling). It was the same story by the time we reached the X-Ray machines. Word of our exploits must have spread, so we had to do a fair bit of greasing palms this time round. We got through

Newcastle airport, same as last time, so it was another successful trip. A couple of weeks after this, my counterparts and I had a falling out over a doorman issue back at work. There were people who were jealous of the money we were making, so they wanted to break this up. The plan these bitches put in place worked, and we decided to go our separate ways.

Despite the breakdown in my business relationship with my cousins, I still needed money to fuel my drug and drink-fueled party lifestyle (it was still the 90's). So, six-weeks later, I decided to go back to Karachi. This time I took two drug mules with me, Mally and Steve. This pair were both local Newcastle lads, who I had known for a while. They were both in their early 20's, with a "no work and didn't want-to-work" ethic. Basically, they just loved taking pills and getting high. Like me, they thought steroid smuggling was a non-heavy offence with a light sentence if we were ever caught.

Once I explained how much money I had made so far, they readily agreed to join me. Besides, they were a couple of wasters with nothing better to do, and I was giving them a paid holiday. The deal was, I would pay all their expenses and give each of them one thousand pounds - once we got back to England with our drugs haul.

We landed at what was becoming my second home, Karachi, and as we were walking through security, I was stopped by an official who introduced himself as, Mr Ahmed. He was medium height, in his late 30's, and wore what was a half-decent suit. Ahmed said he was the Chief Narcotics officer, and he knew all about my operation.

He said, "You just need to pay me one hundred pounds for each suitcase, and you can bring anything you want through."

The weekly wages of an official even this high up were only about one hundred pounds (I thought the salary of a Newcastle doorman was bad).

I said, "Ok," and we shook hands. Even though we acted like business partners, I now had something else to worry about. I was on Ahmed's radar, he knew everything about my flight destinations and times.

The three of us went outside to get our regular taxi, but my pal, Kosa wasn't there like he usually was. Two other taxi drivers came to me and wanted to take us. This pair of chancers knew who I was, so they also knew that if they stuck with me, it meant party time for both of them for the next five-days.

Unfortunately, greed was getting the better of them, and the two drivers started arguing about who would take us. Before the situation escalated to a fist fight, I pulled them apart.

I said to the first driver, "You take me today," and then to the second, "You pick me up tomorrow." A different driver came up to me and said, "You're the king of Karachi."

With this notoriety was being brought to my attention, I tended to agree. I had the Chief of police in my pocket, then the Chief narcotics officer as well. I was enjoying the buzz.

This time round I was going to take Valium back to the UK, as-well-as the steroids. They were a type of Valium called Roche, which came in ten-milligram doses. This time when I arrived from Karachi to the factory in Lahore, they cost me nine-hundred pounds for one-hundred thousand pills. Once I got my haul back home to England, I would sell in bulk at a hundred-and-fifty pounds per-thousand, which gave me a profit of around £10,000 after expenses for one round trip. The dealers didn't care because the street value for them was still one pound per pill – a tidy sum.

Roches came in blister packs, which were difficult to pack for mule smuggling. So, I spoke with the boss, Bashir, at Bang On Traders, and he said he could arrange for all the pills to popped and packed into tubs. I chose to disguise the Valium as B12 vitamin tablets. We got one-thousand tablets in each tub, to a total of one hundred tubs. I felt sorry for the local Lahore kids, who had to pop one-hundred thousand tablets in total. But I was not too sorry because by night, I was being looked after by the girls at the Paradise Hotel.

They had a rotation system, as each time I returned it was for the most part a different set of girls who greeted me. Out of the ten girls here, I knew three. It was a shame Sophia wasn't around, as I had developed feelings for her. I told Mally and Steve if they wanted any sex, they would have to pay themselves (after all I was paying for all other expenses, including food and drink, so anything more was taking the piss).

I put both of them in one room, and I had my own, so they could do their own thing on a night, and I did mine. I didn't like drinking with them, as they weren't my type of people. I wouldn't normally associate with this type of low life. Instead of hanging out with the other two Englishmen, I used to party at night with the girls. I supplied all the drink and pills, and we would all get high together. They didn't charge me for sex, we all had a good understanding going.

A friend of mine from back home had asked me to bring back Nubain, which was a powerful injectable anaesthetic. I had this on me at the hotel. It was my last night in Karachi, I was drinking with three girls in my room. They used to like taking Valium too, so we were mixing them both. I suddenly suggested that we try the Nubain. The girls loved getting high, so they were intrigued by this new drug. I pulled out the vials and set the needle up. It was an intramuscular serum, so I stuck the needle into my fleshy shoulder. After a few minutes, I was on a different level. I thought I was floating. The girls wanted to try it too, so I jabbed all three of them (with different needles of course, I'm not rank). We were all high as fuck now, so I got one of the girls and started kissing her. Then the other two stripped off, and I was into them too. I was stood in the middle of the room with three girls kneeling before me all taking turns to suck my cock. One was licking my balls, one was sucking on it and the other was biting my shaft. I looked down and thought, "Fuck, I truly am the King of Karachi."

The next morning the three of us walked into the airport, and I was feeling confident. The mules, however were nervous, and had the shits that day. I did my best to reassure them I had things boxed off, and I did. My man, Karachi airport's Chief Narcotic's officer was waiting. Ahmed welcomed me like a long-lost friend, before he got security to put all our cases on a trolley.

He led the way past everybody, our bags didn't even get x-rayed. We walked behind him and it was a smooth operation. I felt important. I paid him one-hundred pounds per suitcase, which he insisted was paid in pounds Sterling (probably because he was doing deals with other people) and we went home. Ahmed knew when I would be coming (about every six weeks), and he would always greet me at the airport on arrival. The taxi drivers knew when I would be coming also, and they would always fight over me. After a few trips, I was making serious dollar. There wasn't enough space in my safety deposit box under my bed at home, so I had to change all the twenty pound notes into fifties to make the wads fit inside.

4 RED DOTS

I had to get rid of Mally and Steve, as they looked like shit. They couldn't keep their hands off our product, and not wanting to get personal, but they their personal hygiene was low, which could have drawn attention to us from British security. I sent word, and called out my new mules, who I will call Harry and Michelle. This pair were posing as a tourist couple, and they met me separately at the Paradise Hotel. Harry was a good kid, but Michelle loved herself too much. Harry seemed to be down on his luck. He was my age and I'd known him since we were sixteen-years old. Michelle was a booty call, she was twenty two, small and had a tidy little body. In England, we used to hook up randomly to get high and have sex. She was in a bit of debt, so I asked her to come along to Pakistan with me and make some money. I offered the same deal as the other mules. From her reaction, I could tell she thought this was an excuse to take her on holiday so I could romance her, but she was wrong. I was into smuggling drugs for the bread and where Michelle was concerned I was also happy to get head. But that was as far as it went, no emotional attachment was allowed.

We were in Pakistan in the middle of the job, killing time while we waited for the pills to be packed by Bang On Traders. It was sunny, and Michelle said she wanted to go to the beach, which wasn't far from where we were. We all decided to go, with trusty Kosa as driver.

The four of us got to the beach, which was ok, nothing flash. We put our towels down. There was nobody else sunbathing. Michelle insisted she wanted to strip down to her bikini.

I said, "Ok", but Kosa advised it wasn't a good idea. Michelle stripped off anyway, and the next thing we knew there were about fifty men all around us taking photos of Michelle.

I got up and told them, "Fuck off," but they weren't budging. They had never seen a white girl before, and now they were getting an eye-full of one on her back half-naked in a bikini. Michelle was loving the attention, she'd never had an audience like this. Two cops came over, and they told all the people to move. I thought they were going to order Michelle to cover up, but they didn't. They were quite happy to stand guard and enjoy the show.

"We want to promote tourism, feel free," they said. It was soon time to fly back, and as always my man Ahmed was waiting at the airport to make sure the job always went like clockwork. We got the flights and landed in Newcastle Airport, on the connecting flight from Amsterdam. Michelle, Harry and I were waiting for our bags, but this time they didn't come. I asked the airport staff. It transpired the bags were still in Amsterdam, and they were due come over on the next flight. Fuckin' nightmare for me, but Michelle and Harry were happy, as they were stressing over this bit. Now the bags were missing the pressure was off them.

I said, "Fuck this," and went home. Later I phoned Newcastle Airport, and asked about my bags. They said they had them, but they had opened them and found the pills. If I came to collect them, Customs would arrest me. I was on the radar now so I had to think of a different way to get the gear back to England in future. The dough was too good to give up on. I decided I would bring the pills back to the UK by getting the gear to Spain, and then travelling by train to England through the Eurotunnel. I did a dummy run, and found security checks were minimal.

I soon went back to Karachi with Michelle and Harry. I needed to make up for the last hit, so this time round I got to my base at the Paradise Hotel, and bought thirty thousand ampules of Sustanon and 250,000 Valium. I stood to make seventy-grand profit in Sterling from the lot.

Everything was packed, and we were ready for the journey back to the UK. Karachi airport was smooth as always, then we changed at Amsterdam to get the flight to Alicante in Spain. We would then catch our train to England. We collected our bags at Alicante, and walked to security. I was leading the way. I turned the corner, and seven Guardia Civil were waiting. They had machine guns pointed at me, I had about four red dots shining into my face. I knew then that I was completely screwed.

5 THE FEDS

Interpol had been tracking me. We were cuffed, and our cases were opened up. The heavily armed Feds failed to contain their excitement at the capture of this haul. They were laughing, and looking at me as if to say, "You're fucked." We were taken to the police station, and Harry and Michelle were led to a holding room. Lucky sods. Instead of a cosy room, I was placed outside the main building in a freezing cold container with no windows, and no light. They interrogated Harry and Michelle who both pointed the finger at me.

After a few hours the Feds took me out of the container and into the station. There were four of them, all of a similar stamp and age. They looked like typical Spanish Feds, with their pockmarked faces and greasy black hair. They sat me down, and wanted to know everything. They asked about my flights, how many times have I done this before, have I got property in Spain, and who was I meeting with here? I wasn't meeting anybody in Spain, so I said I was taking my friends back to England. They couldn't understand why I had come through Spain. I made it clear I wasn't going to tell them shit.

I just said, "I'm a bodybuilder, and I need the Valium to sleep." They obviously didn't believe me as they were laughing and cracking Spanish jokes. Then they produced my bag, and started to rifle through it. They pulled out a sleeve of fags which I had bought, and they started handing them out to smoke later. They got out my towels and clothes – these bent Feds were picking what they wanted.

"Whoa what are you doing?" I said. One mean-looking cop put his hand on his gun and said, "Do you want a problem?" I said, "Take what the fuck you want." Then he saw the emerald ring I had bought in Pakistan. He told me to hand it over.

"Do I get a receipt for that?" I said as I handed it over. They all laughed out loud. I hated these motherfuckers, but there was zero I could do. We were put into a holding cell for two days before we were taken to Alicante jail – which I was soon to find out was the worst in Europe. Because they complied, Harry and Michelle were fed and watered, but I got nothing. All my possessions were taken from me, including a large amount of cash, which would have come in useful for legal defence. The three of us were rounded up, and taken to a new holding cell, where the police would decide our fate. This unit was a block of ten cells with bars on the doors. We were all put in separate cells with two other prisoners to share with. They were Spanish and couldn't speak English. The ones I shared with looked like bag heads (junkies). I was getting riled at this point as I didn't know what was going on. I tried asking the screws (prison guards) standing outside, but they insisted they didn't have a clue if I was going to be bailed, or sent to prison. Harry and Michelle were further down the landing than me. I told them that things would be ok if we all stuck with the same story. I was trying to reassure them, but I could see they were stressed out. I don't know what the Feds had told them about what was going to happen, but I knew they would have told them the worst case scenario.

After the second morning a screw came and unlocked us. He announced we were all going to Fontcalent prison. Harry and Michelle's faces dropped, and so did mine. Having all been part of the drugs scene in England, and such was its notoriety that all of us knew of this jail's fearsome reputation. We were immediately cuffed and taken in a van. It was about a half-hour drive. We got out the van, and Michelle was led away. I could see the hurt in

Harry's eyes. I felt bad now. Harry and I were taken to the prison reception and told to strip naked. The screws searched our clothes, then they told us to get showered. We washed and sprayed with a de-licer before being given our jail clothes. Grey pants and a t- shirt. Michelle went to the women's wing, Harry to Modulo 1 and I went to top-security Modulo 4.

The street value of the Sustanon we smuggled was £150,000, the Valium was £250,000, which made the 60 kilos of steroids worth a total of £400,000. This was the biggest seizure of pharmaceutical drugs in Spanish history. It was on the television news and in the papers across Spain. Soon afterwards, news of our bust hit the headlines in England. Suddenly everybody knew who I was. The story being run back home was that Harry and Michelle were totally unaware of what they were carrying, as they allegedly didn't pack their own bags. The media was making me out to be the bad guy.

Harry and Michelle were freaking. Inmates on their wings knew the story, and they were telling the young couple they could get ten years for their part in the caper. The pair of them were now flapping. They were telling the screws they didn't know they were carting drugs. There was a British consulate who visited us, called John. He was a small guy, around five-feet five inches tall with a white beard. John only came to see me once, but he was seeing Harry and Michelle every day. He obviously believed the stories he had read in the papers, so it looked like the British Government was prepared to leave me to my fate. Harry and Michelle were trying to grass their way out and stitch me up. The only option I had left was to help myself. I got word sent to Harry and Michelle's families that this couple of mules were fully aware of what they were doing, and I stressed that it wasn't a good idea to try to stitch me up. After that Harry and Michelle started to comply.

6 BAR NONE

About half the population of Fontcalent Prison were foreign criminals. There were people from all over the world: South Americans, Africans, Europeans, Asians, Russians, every nationality was represented here. I heard about a few British nationals being held, but they weren't in my section of the prison. Because of my size I was immediately placed in the top-security wing, Modulo 4. At the time of my arrival, I weighed sixteen-and-a-half stone, my neck was twenty-inches thick, and arms nineteen inches. The Spanish authorities thought I had money in Spain and might try to escape prison and leave the country. This was bullshit. I had no property or assets in Spain, and the Feds had taken all my cash. I got a lawyer called Juan Carlos who was in his 40's, tall with black curly hair. He had a big fat pockmarked nose. With the money I had sent from the UK, I paid him two-thousand pounds. I was holding onto the hope I was going to get bail in a few weeks, and be out of this hellhole.

I quickly formed a friendship with one of the only people in the wing that could speak a bit of English, a drug dealer called Carlos the Killer. He was about thirty years-old, skinny and not that tall. Carlos was doing sixty-years for two murders, he was HIV positive, and the two men he murdered were both killed by him when he was in jail for another crime. He used to sell smack (heroin) on the wing and nobody fucked with him. A major deterrent for anyone thinking of violence towards Carlos was when you looked in his eyes, there was nothing there - they were just dead. But he and I got along.

Carlos used to smoke heroin, and I started to smoke it with him. I admit the drug quickly took a hold of me. Heroin made me forget I was in prison. It gave me confidence, and made me feel good. At the beginning of a prison term in a place as-dangerous-as Modulo 4, you needed to make friends quickly. When a few of us would take it together, it gave us all a bond. Also, if you share smack with somebody it's only courteous to invite them to your cell when you have some. But when you got hold of the Golden Brown, you don't want to share it. I was getting money sent in by my family, and I was spending it all on smack. I even phoned a few friends from jail, and told them to send me some magazines and put them in a Jiffy bag. The heroin would be hidden in the bubbles of the envelope. Soon my pals in England were too concerned for me to send any more, so this supply stopped. Looking back that was a good thing, as the comedown from heroin was a killer. It used to shrink my stomach so badly I couldn't eat. This made my position in prison ten times worse. The only thing that could make the cold turkey better was more smack.

At this time, I had a few fights, which were all due to lack of ability to communicate with the other inmates, and made worse by my desire for drugs. In particular, the word 'fuck' used to get me into a lot of fights. Early on, I was pissed off and couldn't speak Spanish, so if something wasn't going my way I used to curse, "for fucks sake," or "fuck that." The Spanish lags (prisoners) couldn't understand English on the whole, but the world knows "Fuck" is an insult. So many of the prisoners in my proximity used to think I was directing the insult at them. Carlos used to help me out in these situations, by explaining that I was just swearing generally.

That was the situation when this new guy arrived on our wing. It turned out his name was Manuel. I don't know what the problem was on his previous wing which led to him ending up being sent to us, but he was Spanish and seemed weak and scared, unlike the resident hard cases he was being sent to live with. The next morning Carlos the Killer and I were walking the yard, when we noticed this new guy sitting down crying. I went over to him. I asked Carlos to ask him what was wrong, and Carlos said that a Gitano (gypsy in Spanish) had taken his daily Valium from him. I need to explain that in addition to turning a blind eye to blatant drug-use, the guards gave us anti-depressant pills to keep everyone as calm as possible. I said "Which one took your Valium?" and this fella pointed out Juan. Juan was a big Spanish gypsy with long hair, who was doing a long sentence. He had HIV, which meant I wanted to avoid a fight and possible infection from him, if possible. However, I hate bullies more than anyone else (apart from Feds), so Carlos and I went over to Juan. I told Carlos to ask Juan if he's just taxed (robbed) the new guy.

"Yes. What's it got to do with you?" Juan said.

"Give him his pills back." I said. Juan refused.

"Ok, let's go in the showers." I was expecting him to say no, but instead Juan called my bluff and agreed. He got one of his Gitano pals as a backup, and all four of us walked to the showers. Carlos and I followed them in.

The showers and toilets were combined in one block. There was nobody else within the confines of the slippery tiled walls apart from us. As Juan and I squared up against each other, the Gitano pulled out a knife from his waist. Straight away my pal, Carlos handed me his knife. I had time to quickly study Juan's blade. It was a pen knife blade, about three inches long, with a homemade handle. The shank Carlos had given me was of a similar stamp. I'd never been in a knife fight before, and I didn't know what to do. I was in shock mode. Juan lunged for me and I did move, but still got caught. I was stabbed with the knife on my left hand side below my ribs. Luckily for me it wasn't deep. I immediately countered, striking Juan in the mid-section. He was bleeding, and fell back on his ass. Carlo said, "Give me the knife, and follow me out," so I did. He told me to go walk around the yard while he got rid of the knife. Juan was taken to an outside hospital, and I didn't see him again after that. I heard later that he was ok.

Now my situation was tense. I was scared of getting more years added on my sentence. You could get ten years for knifing someone in jail, but in Fontcalent they slashed each other anyway. I was also weary in case the other Gitanos turned on me. There were about eight on the wing in total, and they were a tight crew. So I asked Carlos to find out what the score was with them, and he did.

He said, "Juan was a bully and people aren't bothered about him." Carlos also reassured me that Juan wouldn't grass me. So after the knife fight, I started to get acknowledgement from the older heads. There were about six of these prison elders here, who the younger inmates respected. They were always either bank robbers, or big time drug dealers. Murderers didn't hold that authority, because they weren't necessarily organised. Just because you had killed someone, didn't make you a leader. Killers held a different sort of respect that was more like fear, which ranked depending on who they had taken out.

After the fight with Juan, the older heads started to say hello to me. They knew I would protect weaker prisoners, and I could hold my own when needed to. Sometimes one or two of them would play a game of chess with me.

7 CHASING JUNK

It was New Year's Eve 1999. We had all been locked up for the night since seven pm. I'd been smoking smack earlier, and I was now on a comedown. I got up in my cell, which was just five-foot by eight. I had a concrete slab for a bed and a thin sponge for a mattress. I looked at myself in a little cracked mirror above the sink, and took a look at what I had become. In just a couple of months, I had gone from having a powerful physique I was proud of, to being a skinny heroin addict. I went into Fontcalent weighing sixteen-and-a-half stone of muscle, but I was now just a feeble twelve-stone bag of bones. When I looked in the mirror, I barely recognised myself. The skin of my face was a greyish colour, and I had black circles under my eyes. I was gaunt and had little energy when I was off the smack. I didn't have the urge to do anything, except to get high again. Two thousand Pesetas would get me high for the full day, and if I could get it I was taking it daily. I was just like all the other smackheads here now. It was a total shock to see what I had become. Carlos and Manolo were the resident dealers, but most of the inmates used to get their heroin smuggled in from friends and relatives attending closed visits. Sometimes there was a lot of it around, and other times it could be totally dry for a few days.

My life had hit rock bottom. I got a letter from my wife telling me her and kids had left me. I realised my shit lawyer Juan

Carlos had failed to bail me. He knew I wasn't going to get bail unless the judges were bribed. In Spain money talks, and this arsehole wasn't far enough up the league to start bribing. He was a total waste of cash and time. In England the drugs I was caught with were classified as class C, which carries a maximum sentence of two-years jail time. I found out, to my shock, that in Spain even a legal drug like the Valium I was caught with was class A (the highest). I was suddenly looking at ten years jail. The Spanish police had taken all my cash off me, one-hundred thousand pounds. I knew if my situation stayed the same I was going to die in this shit pit, either from being killed in a fight or from contracting AIDS. To survive, I needed to keep up my strength. The big problem was the prison menu, which consisted of various stews with meats I couldn't recognise. The main story on the food was, if you were HIV-positive then you could get a job in the kitchens. Those bastards used to spit and do other shit to the food. The veg was always boiled, and was just a mush by the time we got it. A piece of chicken was doled out once a week. When the prisoners working in the kitchen defrosted the meat, they would put it on the floor so the rats could come and take bites out of it. We could see these bites when we got meat on the bone. For breakfast it would be bread and jam. At first I just used to dip the bread in the stews and eat that. I was hardly eating.

The New Year's Eve Millennium Night was one everyone remembers, and it was the shock of realising this milestone that made me reflect on what I had become. I had gone from being at the top of my game by smuggling unprecedented volumes of drugs across national borders, to living in a tiny cell as a junky. I knew then I had to take a grip, as it looked certain I was going to be in Fontcalent for the long-haul. The next day, I packed the smack in, and I have never had it since. That was my turning point, and from then I started to take a hold on my life.

I knew if you were a Muslim you got chicken twice a week and also rabbit. Even though I'm a Sikh, I told the screws I was a Muslim, and that I needed to eat Halal meat. And I got it straight away, no questions asked. With the extra protein I was getting, I decided to pick myself up, create a gym and start training. I used whatever I could find, mainly benches, plastic chairs, old barrels and containers I filled with water or sand. Other inmates soon joined me, and they appreciated the facilities I provided. Training sharpened my mind and improved my moral, but unfortunately the war with the Gitano Juan wasn't quite over. After one grueling session, I was washing my face in the gym sink, when I felt a sudden thud in my back. I turned round, and this big Gitano I hadn't seen before was there looming over me. He looked similar to Juan with long greasy hair. His eyes were bulging, and he gripped a long nail with a handle, dripping with blood. I could feel wetness on my back and turned on him in a rage. I could see the look of shock written on this Gitano face as he looked at me. Maybe he thought after being stabbed in the back, I would have just slumped down. I needed to make the most of his surprise, so that's when I hit him bang on the chin, and put him on his ass. Even in the heat of the moment, I was that paranoid about getting extra years on my sentence that I decided to walk away and leave him. It turned out this guy was Juan's cousin, and apparently that's what Gitanos do for each other.

8 HAVE A GOOD DAY

I was in the top security wing with about forty heads of prisoners. Over half of them were doing life and about the same number of them had HIV through injecting heroin and whatever shit it was cut with. Our wing was also a punishment wing, which meant if you had done something wrong on a different wing of the jail you would get sent to us.

One time this dude called Valencia (after his hometown) was sent over as he had a fight on his wing. He was around five-foot eight inches tall and stocky, in his mid-thirties. To me he looked a bit like the British serial killer and rapist Fred West. He was due to be with us for thirty days. There is a rule where every inmate is allowed a closed visit once a month, so he could have sex with his wife or girlfriend. If you do some good grassing then you could get an extra visit. So every fucker was grassing each other up. I didn't have any visits. This dude, Valencia decided to grass my man Carlos to get an extra visit. The screws found Carlos' stash of drugs, and sent him to the Hole for two weeks. The Hole is a punishment cell eight foot by five, with no windows. You don't get to see anybody in the time you are here. You are opened up for half hour daily, where you can wash in a sink, and walk inside a closed unit. Food is pushed under the door. When Carlos came back everyone was expecting him to make a move on the dude that grassed him, but he didn't do anything all week.

On a Saturday you could get a window visit for one hour, where you can sit opposite your visitors and talk to them through a phone. Valencia had a visit and so did Carlos. On these days everyone, prisoners and visitors alike, were properly frisked, and a metal detector was used, so no knives or other objects could be smuggled into the area. Carlos, Valencia and a few others were taken over to the visiting area, and they were filed into their own cubicles where their families would come on the other side of the glass. The screw's metal detectors couldn't pick up metal if it was inside your body. Carlos went into his cubicle, said hello to his sister who was visiting him, and pulled out a shank (knife, in this case a folding one) from his ass. He then went into Valencia's cubicle where his mother, sister and niece had come to visit him. Carlos stabbed the dude eleven times in his neck and body. Valencia did not stand a chance. He died instantly in front of his horrified family. Valencia was Carlos' third prison murder, and he went to the hole again for two-months.

Once Carlos came back on the wing with the rest of us, he was walking the yard like nothing had happened. He was always cool with me, so I went up to him and said, "Que pasa," which means, "What's happening?" He told me the story in Spanish, which I could understand by this time. Then he explained, "I could have killed him anytime, but I wanted to kill him in front of his mother." I just replied, "Ok, bro. Have a good day."

9 BOOTSO

Bootso was previously held in Fontcalent's biggest wing, Modulo 1, which was home to about eight-hundred inmates in total. He was five foot nine inches tall, stocky with powerful legs. Bootso could speak a bit of English, so he and I developed a friendship after a couple of days. He soon revealed he was with us because he had a fight on Modulo 1, but maybe "fight" is the wrong word. He knocked out his cell mate, because the fella used his razor.

The powerful fighter told me, "I nutted him, then gave him a one-two and he was out cold."

It turned out Bootso was 25 years-old, from Bosnia. He used to be a kickboxer, then turned pro-boxer before he was drafted into the army, but he did not like it. He told me it was boring, as all they used to do was get high all day-long. He eventually went AWOL, and the Feds were looking for him. Apparently it was quite a serious offence if you were absent without leave in the Bosnian service. He was on the run for a few days, when he was eventually stopped by two cops. They demanded his ID, but he didn't have any. He knew he was going to get nicked, so he punched one cop and knocked him out cold. The second police officer shot Bootso twice in the chest. The adrenaline must have kept him going, and in response Bootso took the gun off the cop and shot him. He didn't hang around to see if he was alive or not, but he told me the cop didn't move afterwards.

After getting life-saving backstreet medical attention, Bootso fled to Spain, where he became a pimp. He was a ruthless operator, and used to keep the girls hostage if he felt they had disobeyed him in some way. He got caught when one of the brass cried help from a bedroom window. Luckily for Bootso, he was only charged with keeping hostages in Spain, not for shooting the cop in Bosnia.

This kickboxer had an excellent fighting-style, and he used to share his moves with me. He taught me a lot in the two-months he was there. We used to train from nine-thirty to eleven-thirty each morning, then walk the yard for another two-hours a day. Bootso's legs were very powerful. He used to back-kick the prison wall in the gym, and the whole wall would shake. The vibration would follow into the screws office, and they would look out of the window, as if to say, "What the fuck was that?" Bootso was arrogant and did not get along with anybody else on our wing. He was awaiting bail. He said he had a bent lawyer that would get him out, so he wasn't bothered about making any friends, or avoiding new enemies. I was training with Bootso, when he said he wanted to go to the library. He had only been gone half-an-hour when another prisoner rushed into the gym and told me Bootso had just knocked somebody out in the library. He had been in Modulo 4 for just a few weeks, and the other inmates already hated him, especially the Gitanos. They used to serve the food, and Bootso would take what he wanted from them, which would cause arguments. This tension led Bootso to have his second fight, this time outside his cell verses two Gitanos. He chinned them both.

My dealer, Pirata came to me when I was walking the yard, and he said that the Gitanos wanted to do Bootso in (kill him). He said, if he fucks with them again they were going to stab him. He knew I was his only friend. He was asking me to talk to Bootso to calm down, and get him to behave himself. I said, I would talk to him. I informed Bootso as to what Pirata had said.

He replied, "Fuck him, I'll knock him out as well."

Not the answer I wanted to hear. I was his only mate, so if anything went down I would have to stand with Bootso. He wouldn't change his attitude, so I made sure I didn't leave his side. I got on with the Gitanos now, and I knew I could help diffuse any confrontation between them. Luckily he made bail the next day. We said our goodbyes, and I carried on practicing the Bootso fighting-style. As things would turn out I was to owe him for all he taught me.

10 HOUSE OF PAIN

The gym I had developed was coming on well. I used empty bleach barrels that I filled with water for weights, with bin liners for handles. I had also gotten hold of three broom stick handles, which I taped together to use as a barbell. I also made a punch bag. Officially there was an outside gym, but we rarely got to use it. The screws were lazy ,and they couldn't be bothered to take us there due to all the security measures they had to enforce. The gym screw was a woman, and she liked me. She had seen that I had done a good job on my wing, and people were using my gym every day. I kept it clean and tidy. I asked the female gym screw for some boxing gloves and pads and I got them. With this equipment I could now spar against my training partners.

Soon after the gym was setup, a Russian called Shev came to our wing. He was 25 years-old, six-foot two-inches tall, and of medium build. He thought he was a kick boxer, and did look a bit like the action-star Dolph Lundgren, but far uglier. Shev had a fight on Modulo 1, and his wrist and hand was in a plaster. He said he hit the other kid so hard he had broken his wrist. He had lots of attitude, and insisted he was part of the Russian Mafia. Shev thought he was so tough, that after about two-weeks he decided to take his plaster off. Then he started to train in my gym.

He asked the screws for gloves and then started training on the punch bag. When he finished his bag work, he just threw the gloves on the floor and walked away.

So I said, "Hey, hand the gloves back in."

Shev said, "No. You hand them in."

So I said, "Ok, if that's how you want it then we will put the gloves on and fight here tomorrow at ten o'clock."

He said, "Ok," and walked away as if he was King Kong.

I had been in Modulo 4 for about twenty months now, and I had a few friends. Despite the confrontations I had with their community, my allies were mainly Gitanos and the other Spanish lads. Nobody liked the Russians as they all had attitude, and were racist to anyone more brown than they were. Therefore, the only people the Russians got in with were the Germans. Word was out about the fight tomorrow, and people were buzzing and putting bets on who would win. The Gitanos were winding the Russians up by saying their man was going to end up dead. On the day of the fight I was feeling confident. I had seen Shev training, and he didn't impress me.

We cleared the gym area, and my guys, ten Gitanos and Spaniards, were all standing behind me, covering the screws' window. Shev's guys were behind him, five Germans from the wing, and another two Russians. The screws were looking on with curiosity because they had never seen so many people in the gym before. They knew about the fight and they wanted to watch it too, but they couldn't make it obvious.

We both had gloves on, and it was boxing only. We would only stop if the screws came. All the spectators were excited, and then my man Carlos shouted, "Let's go!"

Shev went to touch gloves, but I just attacked him, moving forward with every punch Mike Tyson-style. He had no option but to move backwards. He ended up against a wall next to his people. I hit him with body shots, then an uppercut.

Carlos cried out, "screws!" so I backed off.

We all tried to act naturally, but it was obvious the screws knew everything. After a few minutes, they walked away, and we started the second round. I knew he couldn't handle my physical strength, so I powered into him again, hitting him with head shots. Shev threw a few shots back, but they weren't hurting. I caught him with a good left. He turned around, and went down on one knee. He was kneeling with his hands up covering his face, with his back to me. I hit him again with another left. My fist went bang on his bad wrist, and I broke it again. He let out a couple of screams. The Russians gang were saying I was out of order for hitting Shev when he was down. They wanted all bets cancelled. But we weren't having it. Shev should have remembered: there are no fair fights in The Can.

11 JONAH?

Karim came to us because he had had fight on his previous wing. He was going to be with us for a month. Karim was only five-foot seven inches, with a slim build, and tight curly black hair. He was an Algerian in his early twenties, but he had lived in Holland for a while, so his English was good. When Karim came over to the wing, he came straight to me. He had heard of my reputation while on his previous wing from my mule Harry, and the other Brits held there. Karim had been promised I would look after him, if I believed his story.

He had been arrested for rape. He said that he knew a prostitute in Alicante, and he had paid her for sex. They had decided to score some smack together. Unfortunately, Karim chose to pay for it by stealing back the money he had given to the prostitute for sex. When she realised what had happened she cried rape. In prison, he seemed scared and wouldn't leave my side. I didn't mind, as he could speak English and I believed his story. However, the other inmates on our wing had realised Karim was in for rape, and many of them wanted to kill him. Because I had taken him under my wing, I was getting pressurised to unfriend him, so he would lose the only protection he had.

I told them his story and explained that I believed him, but they still weren't happy. A gang of four Germans who were on remand for kidnap had the most hatred for Karim. In my opinion they didn't like him because he was Algerian, and the rape issue was just an excuse. Their leader, Marcel approached me in the breakfast line. He was in his late twenties, five-foot ten inches tall, with a stocky build and short black hair. His body was covered in tattoos. This German had the habit of walking about as if he had two invisible microwaves under his arms.

"He's a rapist, why are you defending him?" demanded

39

Marcel. I told him Karim was due in court the following week for his rape trial.

"If he's found guilty, then I will do him in as well," I promised. However, Marcel would not accept this compromise. The rest of his group wanted Karim dead immediately. The whole wing knew what was going down, and the atmosphere was becoming explosive. When the wardens of the jail opened Karim's cell up in the mornings, he used to run straight to my cell and wait for me. He was terrified.

He and I were training in my gym one time. Nobody else would train with us, so we were alone. From the gym window you could see the exercise yard. I spotted the Germans pointing up to our window, clearly planning a move on us.

I said to Karim, "You're going to have to fuck Marcel, otherwise they're going to fuck you."

I told him to break a tile off the gym wall, smash it up into pieces, and put the broken bits in a couple of socks. Then I explained he should go into the middle of the yard, and hammer the German over the head with his new weapon. Karim obediently started to do as I said. He picked up the socks with smashed tiles in it, and walked alone into the yard. I was carefully watching him as he approached the group of four Germans.

Marcel was seated with his back turned. Karim crept up behind him, raised his first tile-filled sock, and struck his enemy decisively on the side of his head. Marcel began to stand up, Karim hit him again, and it was another sweet hit. Blood was gushing from Marcel's head, and Karim instinctively took a step backwards. The other three Germans quickly surrounded him, just as the guards burst on the scene, and marched Karim to a secure unit for his own protection.

Karim was due in court in two days. It was a tense time for me. If Karim was found guilty of rape, then the wing would turn on me. He went to court and the prostitute turned up, and told the truth. So the result was: Karim walked free, and had gotten away with busting the German up at the same time.

12 THE INTER-WING

The communication system between inmates of different wings consisted of throwing batteries over the walls of the wings with messages, drugs or money wrapped round them. Someone from the next wing to ours would throw a battery over with a message, either wanting to buy, or to sell drugs. The sender would get a reply, and then money would be wrapped round the battery and thrown to our side. After the money was received by the supplier, the drugs would be thrown over to the buyer. It was rare that anybody got ripped off as all the prisoners knew each other.

There were two wings adjacent to ours. The first was the double top security wing, where there were only six heads at any time. There were two ETA (separatists) terrorists, and the others were psychopaths so dangerous they weren't allowed to mix with the rest in the top security wing. Carlos eventually ended up here. The other side was known to be, "The Lunatic Wing". They had trees and grass in their yard to give them a better environment for their mental health.

One afternoon after siesta my main dealer, Pirata and I were walking the yard. He was ok with me, as I used to buy my hash from him, but he was still dodgy, hence his name Pirata (Pirate). Pirata used to rip others off, but not me. He knew I had a constant stream of money. He was one of the top heads in the Gitano firm. He'd been in jail most his life, but mostly short sentences. He had HIV, but was always smartly presented, unlike many of the others with the disease who seemed to have given up. Pirata was known to be generous to his friends.

In England inmates walk in a circle, but in Spain we used to walk up and down. A battery came over from the Lunatic Wing, and Pirata picked it up. He followed convention and threw a message back. Then another battery came over, and Pirata sent one back. It was all quiet and everyone continued to walk the yard. All of a sudden a hail of bricks and stones rained down on us. Everyone was diving for cover, but a few of us got hit. The broken-up bricks kept just coming. Then when the guards tried to stop the lunatics they got stoned as well. On each corner of the wings was a tower where a guard was stationed, armed with a pump-action shotgun. The tower guards had to fire shots at the lunatics to make them stop their bombardment. I heard later that the lunatic wing had taken a garden wall apart to bombard us. Pirata admitted that he had received a message from the Lunatic Wing requesting smack, and he did send a message back saying he had some for them. But Pirata didn't send the drugs over. He bumped (stole from) the other party. When it was over we all found it hilarious, apart from the ones that got injured, and the lunatics probably.

13 WOLF

This story is about Lobo, which means "Wolf" in Spanish. The other prisoners called him this because he was a little hairy fucker. Lobo came to our wing because he had been caught selling smack on another wing. He was sent over to us indefinitely. When new people used to come to Modulo 4, they would be scared because Fontcalent was considered the worst prison in Spain, and our wing was the roughest wing there - apart from the Lunatic Wing that is.

Lobo was only small with a pleasant little face, but I will say again for emphasis: he was hairy as fuck. He looked timid when he came into the yard, as others knew he was a dealer, and he was scared of getting taxed by them for his possessions. I went over to Lobo, said "hello", and asked where he was from. I said this in Spanish because I could talk a little by this time. He told me "Columbia", and said that he had once lived in the West End of London while working as a coke dealer. Once I realised he could speak English, him and I hit it off. He was a funny guy, and looked a bit like Robin Williams.

In Spain Lobo was doing a nine-year stretch for international drug smuggling. The little guy started to train with me. He told me how he made his living by swallowing cocaine packages, and bringing them to Spain from Columbia. He said that he could swallow one-and-a-half kilos, and put an extra kilo up his ass. When he eventually started living in Spain, he was bringing hashish over from Morocco in exactly the same way. The Columbian's method was to get his hashish, wrap it up in carbon paper and place the packet in a condom. This meant the drugs wouldn't show up on airport x-ray machines.

He and his mate went to Morocco, where they could buy their hash cheap. They each swallowed the one-and-a-half kilo, and both put a kilo up their asses. As they were coming through airport security, officers stopped Lobo and took him to get x-rayed. Nothing showed up from the scan, but the Feds were not convinced. They locked-up Lobo, knowing he had to take a shit eventually. Then they would nick him. The determination of the Spanish customs to pin something on him meant Lobo knew someone must have grassed him up. He was locked up for a few hours and soon it was early in the morning. He decided he had to take a shit, and out came all the hash. Lobo quickly pissed on the packages, to wash most of the shit off them. Then he re-swallowed each packet. In the morning the screws opened him up from his cell, and found no hash. Legally they couldn't hold him any longer, so they had no choice but to let him go. Lobo said it was a choice of either re-swallowing the hash covered in his piss and shit, or facing three years in jail. To me this was a fair statement.

Another time Lobo and his mate went to Morocco, swallowed their hash, and brought it to Spain. The pair went to Lobo's home to excrete the drugs. His mate couldn't have a shit, because it was hurting him too much when he tried. So they waited. Two days passed, and this guy was in serious pain. Lobo gave him some smack to ease the agony, but this guy was still screaming and begging Lobo to take him to the hospital. Lobo said if they agreed to do that his mate was going to get three-years in prison. Lobo's mate said he was not bothered - he would do the jail time. He just wanted someone to make him shit. Lobo came up with an idea. He put his mate in the bath. Lobo then stuck his fingers up his friend's ass. He felt around, and realised one of the blocks of hash his friend had swallowed was lying sideways across his anus. This was blocking everything up. So Lobo had to stick his full hand up his mate's ass to dislodge the block of hash. He said his pal was squirming and screaming, but Lobo did it and his mate shat all the hash out. Lobo said they had to sell the hash at half-price because it stank so badly of shit.

14 WOMEN'S WING

The women's wing housed about forty heads. They were mainly Gitano wives who had taken the blame for their husband's activities. There were also two scouse girls (from Liverpool, England) there called Lisa and Lesley. They looked after Michelle for me, and all three were sharing a pad together. The two scouse girls' story was they were bringing back cocaine to England. Lisa and Lesley had done it a few times before, by wrapping the coke around their waists. However, the last time they attempted to smuggle the powder, a small amount of aluminum foil was "mistakenly" left in the coke, and the Spanish metal detectors picked it up at the airport. It turned out the ladies were set up so as to distract the Feds from a bigger load, which was going through customs at the same time. The scouse girls had three kilos in total, but by the time it went to court there were only two kilos left. The dirty bastard police took a kilo, but Lisa and Lesley weren't complaining as they ended up with nine-years each when they could have gotten a lot more. They had been inside three-years by-the-time I met them.

Michelle wrote to me and told me about Lisa and Lesley, so I told her to hook the fittest one up for me, and so she did. Soon me and Lisa started to write to each other daily. After a few weeks we decided to apply for a window visit. There were loads of couples in this jail, and every Thursday each pair got to meet each through a window. Lisa and I got the approval, as I was single at the time and so was she. We had to show proof of our relationship through letters written to each other, and we had plenty. Thursday came and I was looking good, apart from loads of cuts on my head by the shit jail razor I had to use to shave my head. I was tanned and at my fittest, so I was feeling confident. Lisa was looking good. I was surprised. She was twenty-four, and had a fit body. She wore a tight white top with no bra. I was getting excited. We had a good laugh together, as we already knew each other through our letters. Also, it was Lisa that had persuaded Michelle not to grass me for using her to smuggle drugs, so I owed her one.

I used to look forward to Thursdays, and we had a good time every visit. Sometimes we would get our bits out when the screws weren't looking. It was brilliant, and it did make my time there more bearable. After six-months of window visits we were allowed to apply for a closed visit. This meant a room with a bed, and nobody would get to see in. So we both applied and we got the permission approved. I was nervous when the day of the visit came. Lisa was already in the room and the screws locked the door behind me. We could hear them listening and giggling outside. That's all I'm going to tell you, except to say the visit was immense, and we couldn't wait for the next one. Like I said before, if you grass people up you can get an extra visit, but if you do extra work then you can get an extra one too. So I said to the screws, if I cleaned up the gym area daily, then would they give me an extra visit? They said, yes if I did a good job. I made sure it was a fuckin good job. Lisa was doing the same on her wing, and both wings were gleaming. We were seeing each other every two weeks. We had these visits for about six-months. Then Lisa's transfer came to Madrid. She was going to a much better jail, so it was a good move for her. Of course I was sad when she went, but at least we got to enjoy ourselves for a while.

15 THE CORNER TABLES

At mealtime, the corner tables were the best one as nobody could stab you in the back. Manolo sat on one corner table. He was a fit and good-looking kid in his early thirties. He was notorious. Manolo was a bank robber, and while on the job he was known for taking people hostage. Manolo even took a policewoman hostage once. He'd had shoot outs with the Feds, and would shoot anybody else who got in his way. He was doing thirty-years in total, and had completed about eight by the time I met him.

On the other corner table was Peru. He got his name because he was from Peru, and he was in his fifties. He wasn't particularly tough, just respected. He was a big-time cocaine trafficker, and was well-connected. He was doing nine-years for coke. Peru was an educated guy.

In Spain the max it seemed you got for cocaine was nine years, and weed four-and-a-half years, no matter what the amount. There were people caught with tons, and others caught with just a kilo, yet they were all doing nine-years. During mealtime, I would sit with two Germans. They were brothers and they were ok, not like the other racists from their country. One morning we were sat at our table having our daily bread and jam. One of the Germans, David, and I were arguing over a plastic knife. My knife was newer, and he was saying it was his. We argued for a while, but I kept the knife and started to spread jam on my bread with it. Next thing I knew, as I was looking down at my plate, David punched me in the face. I got hold of him, and took him to the floor. Tables and chairs were flying everywhere, also everybody's coffee, bread, and jam were being tossed around. We were rolling on the floor. I couldn't get a good grip of David, so I stuck my thumb in his eye. He started squealing just when someone shouted, "screws!" I let go of David, and told him we will fight in the toilet.

It was supposed to be a toilet for the yard, but people used it to fight inside, or take smack inside. I wrapped my hands in a long bandage I had made previously from a bed sheet. I was ready to fight, went to the toilet, and waited for David to enter. All the other prisoners could see what was happening, as they were all walking the yard. David came in, and said he didn't want to fight me because he couldn't see out of one eye. Everyone saw him back down, and so did Manolo the bank robber from his corner table. Dinner-time came, but I didn't really want to sit at the same table as David. Luckily for me Manolo came over and said I could sit at his table. He never let anybody sit with him normally. This was my step-up the pecking order.

16 BREAKOUT

Omar was awaiting sentencing for cocaine smuggling. He was a big time Algerian dealer, in jail for one year by-the-time I first met him, and was expecting nine years in total like me. Omar had a good position in Modulo 4. He was in charge of the economato (shop), which on our wing was very basic, but still good to make a profit from. You could buy water, cigarettes, shampoo, and a few other simple products. I had only been on the wing a few days when I first met Karim, and we kicked off a friendship. He could speak four languages including English. He told me about himself and how he was known as "The Ghost" on the outside. He would do big drug deals and nobody would ever know who they were dealing with. There was a German, Artur who also worked at this shop under Karim. They both got this job as they were considered responsible prisoners by the screws. Artur was the brother of my friend, David who I had fought with over the plastic knife (it was all cool after a few days). They were both over six-foot, but what separated them was, Artur, the youngest, was the one with intellect. David was not really a thinker. It seemed to me like Artur had to look after his older brother.

I began to sit with Artur at meal times, and we formed a friendship, despite the fact I didn't get along with the other Germans. These brothers were different to their countrymen crew, as they mixed with everyone. They weren't bad guys - they were just trying to make dollar. Crime was the obvious answer to making cash for those with little intelligence, or a lack of education. Artur and his brother were drug dealers who had escaped from a prison in Germany and fled to Spain, where they got caught. The other Germans used to look at them as idiots, so neither group was on speaking terms. Artur, Omar, Manolo, and I had cells that were all next to each other above the shop.

As my friendship with Omar grew, he began to open up, and eventually he told me that he was planning to escape. The Algerian asked if I wanted to go with him. Artur wasn't prepared to leave David on his own, and had declined to take part. So I would have to take the job Omar originally had planned for Artur. The screws allowed Omar and Artur to stay in the shop to stock take, while all the rest of us were on association. Association is where inmates can mingle in the main hall. This period is after our evening meal, from six-thirty to eight o'clock. Most inmates preferred to be in their cells at this time, because as the evening wore on, there were always fights and arguments breaking out. But there was a TV there, and we could play chess.

This was what was going down: Omar and Artur spent this ninety-minutes daily, hacking a hole through the wall of the shop to the outside world. It was the only wall we had access to that was external to the whole jail. Once through the wall, we just had to avoid getting shot by the screws in the towers placed at each corners of the prison complex. Foncalent was an old jail in the mountains, and there had been a few escapes here in the past. Omar and Artur were using a metal weight disc they had stolen from the prison gym to hack through the wall. The hole was covered-up by a broken refrigerator. They used to move it out of the way to begin work on their hole.

The plan seemed a bit fickle, and I wasn't totally convinced that it would work. Manolo was supposed to go also, but he wasn't allowed to work as he was considered high risk. Omar pointed out that I was looking at nine-years, the same as him. So why didn't I go with him? The plan was this: Artur would stop working at the shop, and I would apply to replace him. I didn't make particular trouble for the screws, so we knew this wouldn't be a problem. We would continue to dig the hole together, and when everyone was on association we would make a run for it. If we dodged getting shot, there was only a small wall we had to climb. Once we were past that wall, Omar would have a driver waiting to take us to the nearby town of Alicante, where we would go our separate ways.

This was a daunting prospect for me. If I survived and made it to town, I knew I couldn't return to England and remain free. This was the factor I couldn't handle. I had kids, and my family was too important to me. This plan was alright for Omar, as he had connections in Portugal and Algeria. I had fuck all. I told Omar I couldn't escape, as I couldn't handle being on the run for the rest of my life.

My long-term plan was that I would await sentencing, then apply for a transfer to a jail in England. This was going to be Her Majesty's Prison Belmarsh, in London. I made enquiries about this process, and found out that I have to be sentenced in Spain first, which could take over two-years. Then I could apply for a transfer, and that could take up to three-years to come through. This was the only option I had. Besides, I didn't fancy getting shot at. I reassured Omar I would help him as much as I could. I used to go to my cell after my evening meal, and not stay downstairs for association. Once in my cell, I could hear banging below me. I used to fear for him at these times, but the screws' office was away from the shop, so they couldn't hear. This went on for a few weeks.

A month later Omar came to my cell, and said that he was going out that night. We had to synchronise our watches, and at exactly seven-thirty pm, I was to stage a fight with Artur to distract the screws, while Omar made a run for it. By seven twenty-five pm, Artur and I were in the association room along with Manolo, and about fifteen other heads. I told Manolo what was going down. He was gutted he didn't have this chance, because he was doing a thirty-year stretch. As agreed Omar was in the shop on his own at this time. It was now seven twenty-eight pm. Artur staged an argument with me over what channel to watch on the TV. I threw a chair at the burly German, and in return he threw a table at me. Then I went for him, but missed my punches on purpose. We took it to the floor, where we were wrestling with each other amongst the tables and chairs. The screws burst onto the scene wielding batons, and we let them break us up. Just at this moment I heard gunshots outside. All the cons knew this meant only one thing: a breakout. The screws who were restraining Artur and I knew it as well. They dropped the two of us and all back-healed, running for the main exit doors.

"Omar has made a run for it!" shouted Artur.

All the cons were cheering and shouting, but in the corner of my eye, I noticed Manolo looking quite sullen. Everybody wanted to know if Omar had managed it. After about five-minutes the screws came back, and said it was going to be bang-up for everybody. Cons were asking the screws if he had got away, but they didn't say anything. I knew from the look on their faces that Omar had escaped.   My emotions were mixed. The screws knew that Artur and I had staged the fight, so we expected repercussions. Artur 's cell was next to mine and despite the stress, we gave each other a high-five on the way to get locked up. The following day, Omar's escape was on the newspaper and television. The reports said he was a notorious drug dealer not to be approached. He had got away. I couldn't believe it, and a strong part of me wished I had gone with him. All the cons were buzzing that he had pulled it off. A week later I got a postcard from Portugal, signed Ghost. I was happy for him, but gutted about my position. He had fuckin balls.

Six months later, I was going to the outside gym with other heads when I saw Omar cuffed and being marched back into Modulo 4. Omar physically looked the same as when he was here before, but I saw sadness in his eyes. I knew he couldn't really hack jail. He enjoyed the big life too much. The screws were putting him on the other side of the wing with the double category A prisoners (terrorists and psychos). He passed close to me. I said, "What the fuck?" He replied, "I came back to Spain to collect a debt. The guy didn't want to pay, so he grassed me up. Such is fuckin life."

17 MANOLO

Manolo taught me a lot about the Spanish legal system. He was intelligent, but a total thug at the same time. Manolo used to smoke weed every day, and he got me smoking it too. We used to do our own thing in the mornings, then after siesta we would hook up in the yard and get stoned. He told me about his life. Manolo robbed banks from the age of eighteen. He robbed a few over four-years, and eventually he got caught. They gave him twenty-years. He escaped after one-year, and robbed some more banks. His mistake was that he stayed in Spain, and he was caught again after six-months. They sentenced him to ten more years in prison.

A few weeks before he was due in court, Manolo began planning another escape attempt. His cousin, Juan (in Spain nearly every fucker was called Juan or Jose) also sat on our wing. The pair of cousins were up in court together. Juan was a coke dealer doing the standard nine-years. Manolo had managed to get hold of a key for his handcuffs, which he showed me. It was small and gold in colour. I figured he must have bribed a screw, but I didn't ask. His plan was: when they took him and his cousin to court, his cuz would fall on the screws, and Manolo would make a run for it. It didn't really sound like a well thought-out plan to me, but who was I to say?

Manolo still had a few weeks left before his court date, so he was helping me with my case. He told me my lawyer was shit, and I needed to get a bent (corrupt) one instead. He kindly hooked me up with his own lawyer.

One morning, I was walking past the toilet in the yard when I saw somebody slumped on the floor. I went over, and it was a friend of mine called Jose. He was about forty, small and skinny with HIV. Jose had a long sentence, so he was going to die in jail. He had lived in London and we used to have a laugh. Crouching next to him, I tried to bring him round, but he was unconscious. I saw he had been injured, like he had been bashed up. I was angry because this was a liberty. I shouted in the yard, "Who the fuck has done this?" Nobody would speak, so I went and asked around. It turned out a slimy Gitano called Gato (which means "Cat") had done it. He thought he was big time because he had been shot four-times. Jose was late with payment for smack, so Gato had bashed him.

"Fight me I'm more your size," I said to Gato while we stood in the yard.

"Ok, but only a knife fight - I can't fight you straight," he said. This pissed me off, because I really wanted to fuck him up, but I knew he would come stab me in the back.   So, I went to Manolo and told him the story. He said he will sort it, as the Gitanos wouldn't dare stab him. Manolo and I went to the yard, and Manolo started shouting in Spanish. I could only make out the swear words. The whole yard stopped and listened, then Gato walked forward. Manolo took him into the toilets to smash him up. Manolo walked inside first, and Gato followed. I looked inside from the yard. Like lighting, Manolo hit Gato with a straight right. The Gitano staggered back, but Manolo got a hold of his collar, and swung him round so he landed on the floor. Manolo then kicked him in the face twice. Gato lay curled up. Manolo walked coolly out.

The day of the escape came, and we said our goodbyes. I knew I would never see Manolo again. I thanked him for all help he gave me. He was feeling confident, and was in a good mood. He showed me the key in his mouth, and he said he was going to open the cuffs in the van. As soon as the doors of the van were opened his cuz was going to jump on his screw, and Manolo was going to take a gun off one of the other screws. Manolo said if he needed to shoot anybody he would do it.

As expected I never saw him after that. But I heard later that Manolo got the cuffs off in the van, but his cousin, Juan bungled his part. He couldn't get the screw's gun, and was overpowered. They didn't let him come back on the wing. They just came for his stuff, and took him to another jail. Now that Manolo had gone, I got the corner table. It might have been by default, but I still got it.

18 FACE

Now that I had the corner table, I would get instant recognition from new inmates. I would also get the first option of any food that was going spare. Once everyone had been served, the Gitanos, who did the serving would shout, "Indio!" and I would walk up, and take what I wanted. Everyone else had to stand behind me. If it was chicken, I would take about six pieces and eat them over the next few days. In winter it was ok to keep food. In the summer it would get sweaty, but I would eat the chicken anyway. It was the only decent protein we used to get.

Because I was getting surplus food, I decided to do some good with it. I started to feed the jail pigeons. They were all skinny and lacked proper nutrition, so I started giving them an assortment of meat three-times a day. They would wait in the yard below my window at regular times, like clockwork. After a couple of months they were getting big, and I was proud of them. People used to throw batteries at them, but once I took them under my wing, all violence against pigeons stopped.

Now that I was established, I became the money lender on the wing. It worked like this: if you borrowed one-thousand Pesetas, you would pay back fifteen-hundred on the following Monday morning. I would take something of value to hold until the money was paid. Monday mornings were fuckin' crazy. Lots of people had lent money to pay for drugs, and everyone would stand in a queue to pay. For the record, I didn't get any money sent in to me from the outside. I made all my money in Modulo 4. Screws would stand watching as people got their money through the window, then instantly the lenders would pounce on them, and take what they were owed. Most of the time it would be everything the borrower had. The screws would watch and do nothing. Sometimes people just got straight taxed. That's right their money was simply taken from them by someone harder than them.

I made a fair bit of cash considering where I was: in the worst wing, in the worst jail in Spain and Spanish jails were the worst in Europe. So I figured I'm in the worst place in Europe, and if I can make money here, I can make money anywhere. I could speak Spanish by this time, so I studied Spanish drugs laws. In Spain it works like this: they have Class B, which is cannabis. Everything else is Class A. I had 250,000 tablets, with ten-milligrams of diazepam in each tablet. So even though my drugs were no worse than cannabis in England, in Spain they worked out I had two and-a-half kilos of a Class A drug, which is worth nine-years in prison. My first lawyer was full of shit, so once I hooked-up with Manolo's lawyer, I could see he was good. He said that judges take bribes, and we had a case for expulsion so I could get my nine-years reduced to four and-a-half years. I told him to go for it.

19 CHASING DOLLARS

Inmates could get up to 10,000 pesatas sent in each week. This was a ridiculous figure as there was hardly anything to buy from the economarto. But you could spend money on phone calls. Some people were never off it. We had one phone for the whole wing. There was always a queue, and always fights. I used the phone for the first few months, then I couldn't be bothered with the wait. I would rather walk the yard.

When I was on the outside everyone wanted to jump on the Chet Sandhu Express. When the train crashed, the passengers didn't even come to see if the driver was ok. I demanded some sort of security for the money I lent. I made it clear to my "customers" I needed something to hold, for example a Walkman, a watch, or decent clothing. All the prisoners who borrowed money had drug problems, which made them ideal punters.

Soon I had three or four regulars who would borrow money every week. It was a viscous circle. Once they paid their debt, they were totally skint, so they would have to borrow off me immediately to afford their drugs. They were addicts who couldn't break the circle, so they came back to me time-and-time again. I would also get a steady stream of random cons borrowing money for drugs. Manolo and Carlos the Killer were the main dealers. If someone wanted drugs from them and didn't have money, they would point him in my direction. In return for giving their punters money to buy drug from them, they would give me hashish. We had a good thing going. The screws knew what was going down, but they didn't interfere as drugs kept the heads pacified. So I didn't need to ask my family to send money in to me. I told them I could survive on my own.

At times, my cell was full of goods. I had radios, Walkmans, watches, trainers, track suits, jewelry, and anything else of value. After a few months, I was pretty flush, and I had money to buy anything I wanted within the walls of Modulo 4.

There was a Belgian guy called Dudu who was in for the murder of his wife and her lover. He was doing thirty years. Dudu was a decent guy, but liked to smoke hash a lot. He borrowed one-thousand pesetas from me to buy his hash from Manolo. For security he gave me his Walkman to hold. Once Monday came around, Dudu went to collect his money from the screws' office. This was a window like at the post office. Unfortunately for him, Dudu's father had forgotten to send him any cash. He explained this to me, and said it would have to be next week now. I didn't charge Dudu any interest, as he was a good bloke and not a Con like most of the others. His crime was a crime of passion. So to keep me happy Dudu was greasing round me a bit. To impress me, he told me that he could contact spirits from the dead. I was intrigued, and listened to his stories. One night Dudu suggested that we do a Ouija board. I was up for this, so we asked my mate Carlos the Killer and Cassilas, who I had named after the Real Madrid goalkeeper. He was a good goalie, and he was in for murder too. I asked Manolo if he fancied doing the Ouija board, and he said, "Fuck that. I ain't sitting with peasants," which meant he thought it was a backward folk practice.

Later that night the four of us, Dudu, Carlos, Cassilas, and I stayed down for Association. We took a table and four chairs into the showers. We wrote out the alphabet and numbers on pieces of paper. Dudu placed all the letters and numbers in a circle on the table, and put a plastic glass face down next to them. I was excited, but a bit freaked out. I was about to summon people from the dead with three convicted murderers in the jail showers, where quite a few people had already been killed.

We all put our middle fingers on the cup, and Dudu started to talk in Spanish with his eyes shut. He asked if anybody was present. To my amazement the cup started to move. I looked at the others, and nobody was dragging the cup. It was moving on its own. It spelt out Jesus, which was a common Spanish name. Dudu went into a deep trance, and was mumbling. I couldn't understand him, and then the cup went to the number six three-times. The number of The Beast, El Diablo, the devil. Now I was freaked and so was Cassilas. He jumped up, and said he had seen enough. Carlos also said he was heading off.

Dudu said, "The spirit is bad, but he's a liar also."

Carlos told me to get up. He said, if I didn't the spirit could stay with me. Personally I wouldn't have minded a bit of company in my cell, but in the end I decided to get up too.

The next day, I told Dudu to get me some Valium from the doctor, so I could sell them to pay some of his debt off. We both stood in the queue to be seen in the morning. There were about fifteen heads in the queue. I was the fifth line, when a screw (this one was a cunt), came up to me and said go to the back of the queue.

I said, "Why?"

He just looked at me, and pulled his baton out. He pointed to the back of the queue. Then he told two Algerians to go to the back too. I knew he was sending anyone brown-skinned to the end because he was a racist. I looked at him, reached down into my trousers, and got a hold of my cock. I moved it around a bit, which was a gesture mortally insulting to the Spanish. I slowly walked to the back, and so did the Algerians. Then the screw pointed to a black guy from Nigeria, and told him to stand behind everybody.

In Spanish jails the racism normally works like this: the white Europeans are at the top of the pecking order. Then in descending order you've got Gitanos, Arabs and the rest of Asia. At the bottom there were black people. This included blacks who had grown up in the West. It didn't matter where you were from - in jail, if you were black you got treated like shit. We waited in the queue. Dudu got seen, but the last five didn't, including me. I was very surprised by how blatant this treatment was, but you just got to wipe your mouth, and get on with it.

One time I lent a Spanish guy called Murcia (named after his hometown) one-thousand pesetas. He was young, and he was a good kid who used to do a bit of running around for me. Murcia had the misfortune of being half-Spanish and half-Gitano. Neither the Gitanos, nor the Spanish would accept him. He'd been in jail most his life for robbing. He also had a hair lip, and was an orphan, so nobody sent him money in. Murcia had to hustle to make a dollar.

I lent him the money, but I didn't take any security, as he had nothing of any value anyway. I felt sorry for him, and I think he realised this. I gave him three-weeks to pay, but he didn't pay me. He had borrowed money off other people, and had paid them off. So when he didn't pay me it was a direct, "Fuck you."

Murcia had mistaken my kindness for a weakness. He was on punishment for a week for getting caught with a small lump of hash. He was kept in his cell in isolation for a week. Once his punishment ended, he came onto the yard. As I watched Murcia, it was obvious he owed a couple of people money. I knew he must have paid them, as they laid off him. He must have taken me for a soft touch. He didn't smoke heroin, so I couldn't understand how he had gotten into such debts. I went up to Murcia, and asked when he was going to pay me. He said Monday, as he was owed money from another prisoner, which was due then.

Monday came, and he avoided me all morning. Other people knew he owed me money, so I couldn't let this go. He was just a kid down on his luck, and in truth I wanted to let him off, but if I did this I would lose my rep and my livelihood. If the others saw this they would have taken the piss too. It was all about saving face.

After siesta I was walking the yard, when I spotted Murcia walking in, head bowed. I squared up to him and he was looking nervous. I stuck out my right hand to shake his hand. He shook it. I got a hold of his thumb with my left hand and bent it backwards until I heard the crack. He let out a whimper, but not too much. I had to break his thumb to save face, even though I hated doing it. I was a bully now, but sometimes you have to administer violence to survive in an environment like this.

20 PUNISHMENT

We'd just been opened up after our siesta, and as usual I would make my way to the yard. I was doing my normal laps, when I noticed a new con arrive. He was a black guy, with short dreadlocks, medium build. He was about thirty-five years-old. When someone new used to come on the wing, I would always be cool with them at first. I walked over to him as he stood near the main door next to the screw's office. I said, "Que pasa?" (what's happening?) as I offered him a cigarette to make him feel welcome. If you gave a stranger a fag in jail, it was quite a big thing. But I was the money lender there by this time, so I was flush with cash and I could afford to live extravagantly. I asked him where he was from, he said, "Rhodesia." In jail you often get given the name of the town or country you are from, so that was his name now.

The Rhodesia dude took the fag, and I sparked him up. He had a massive pink tongue, and when he took a draw on the fag, his whole mouth would open up then his massive tongue would come out to catch all the smoke. He didn't look normal to me. So I said, "Cool, Rhodesia. I'll see you around," and walked back the way I had come. I thought he would have followed me to walk the yard, but he didn't. He stayed where he was.

A Gitano called, Commer-Commer came to walk the yard with me. His name meant "eat-eat", as he was always eating. He had a big pot belly, even though he was a regular heroine user. He and I were friends. He was in his forties, and had been in jail most his life doing shitty sentences. Commer-Commer had HIV, and he used to get extra supplements because of this. He got extra milk, biscuits, and lots of other good stuff. He used to sell me all his supplements daily in exchange for cigarettes. We had a good thing going - he was also my eyes and ears across the wing. I only spoke with him in Spanish. To me he was a good guy, but the other Gitanos used to take the piss out of him. When this happened, he used to come to me for help.

"That black guy is no good, don't speak with him," Commer-Commer warned me. Then he told me about Rhodesia.

Apparently he was previously jailed for raping a young girl. He'd only been out about six months, and he'd raped and eaten a seven-year-old girl. The whole wing was buzzing with this news.

Commer-Commer got this information from the screws who had told certain cons who Rhodesia was. The policy was: if the rapist is white, then the screws don't say anything about this to the other prisoners. If you were black, Arab or Asian, it was guaranteed the whole jail would know what you did, and who you were.

I could see certain firms getting their heads together to decide the fate of this Rhodesian guy. The older heads were conspiring and the Germans were all looking very serious, although this was probably because he was black over him being a rapist killer. We were in the yard for ninety-minutes, when we were filed-up to be counted before dinner. Nobody would stand in the same line as Rhodesia, so he stood by himself at the end. Everybody filed in to queue for food, and Rhodesia was hanging by himself at the back. Then Peru, one of the older heads, came walking out of the hall with a table and he put it in the yard.

"You can't eat with us, so eat in the yard," Peru said to Rhodesia. The other cons were shouting and cheering.

I was standing to the back of the queue, close to Rhodesia and I could see he was starting to look nervous. A screw came out and put the table back inside. They wanted Rhodesia to take a beating for eating close to other prisoners. Rhodesia looked at me as if I was the last chance ranch. I was the only one who had spoken to him civilly so far.

I held his gaze a few seconds, and I felt a bit sorry for him. However, I thought to myself, "You're not like me, you're a deranged animal." But you can still feel sorry for a deranged animal before it takes a hiding.

I turned away, and went to the food line. I got my meal and walked to my table in the corner, which was still the best table in the house. I sat down and lit a fag. Rhodesia got served and there was one empty table on the side, so he went to it and sat down. My dealer, Pirata was staring at him, while he sat with the other Gitanos. He was a ringleader, and the others were waiting for him to make a move before they did anything. Pirata was on a crutch. There was probably nothing wrong with him, he just wanted to use a fake injury as an excuse to stay in his cell and get high.

Pirata got this crutch, and walked up behind Rhodesia, who was sat hunched over his plate eating. Pirata lifted up the crutch and brought it down on Rhodesia, striking him sideways across the head. The crutch was aluminum, and it just wrapped itself around this rapist killer's head. At this point, all the other eight Gitanos, jumped-up and were punching and kicking Rhodesia. Then the Germans and Russians got tables and chairs, and they were bouncing them off him. They didn't want to punch him, as he was probably HIV positive. The Gitanos weren't bothered because most of them were positive anyway. In total, there were about fifteen people ferociously beating on him. I sat back, and watched.

I never liked to get involved in mob beatings. The older heads hung back too. The veterans didn't get involved in things like that. Instead, it was normally left to the lower-ranking cons to execute this type of punishment. There were tables and chairs being flung all over the canteen. Even people just sat eating their food were getting hit. I could see the screws watching with approval through the office window. A bloodied Rhodesia somehow managed to get up, and he made a run for the screws' window. Nobody followed him. The prison guards came out laughing, and took Rhodesia to the segregation wing. We knew he would then go to a different jail, where he would receive this welcome all over again.

21 GG

My friend Manolo and I were walking the exercise yard after siesta, when we noticed a new fish enter the wing. He was a Gitano in his mid-twenties, small with long black hair, of camp appearance and quite smartly dressed for a Gitano, who were normally fairly shabby. The Gitanos were quite dark-skinned with long black hair. In Modulo 4, they were all related, and most of their wives were also in jail. This one walked towards the other Gitanos, who were sat in the shade in the corner of the yard. I could see some of them sniggering when he walked over to them. They didn't shake his hand, and I could see them having a conversation. Then he walked away from them, and sat in the shade by himself. When it was time for food he sat with a couple of Algerians. It was obvious the other Gitanos weren't taking to him as he was homosexual. That's when the prisoners gave him the name GG (gay Gitano).

GG formed a friendship with a Spanish guy called Pedro, who I thought was probably gay. GG had a visit from his family, and they bought him new trainers and tracksuits. He also got a fair bit of hash and some heroin too. This meant after the visit all the Gitanos who had rejecting him before were around him trying to be his best friend. GG was sat with them in the yard. They were all getting high together. However, as soon as the drugs ran out life was back to the normal run of rejection for GG.

We soon got another new fish on the wing, a Moroccan guy from Modulo 1. He called himself Rio, but he thought he was a badass, so I renamed him Fuck Norris (from the legendary action film star Chuck Norris). I used to call him Norris to his face (he used to say, "I'm Rio, bro." I used to reply, "Yeah, same thing").

Fuck Norris was sent to us as punishment for fighting on his wing. I had to admit this Moroccan was in good condition, and he was a kick boxer. He had long curly black hair, and it always looked greasy. He was about twenty-five. For the first few days, he was quiet and nobody really noticed him. Then he started to open up a bit, and came to train at our gym. He was fast, but lacked power. We did the pads together, I felt his best shots and they didn't bother me. He felt mine too, but I was taller and heavier, which is why he refused to spar with me. To make up for it he used to do flying kicks in the yard to show off. He did look impressive. Norris then started to hang out with GG. A lot of Moroccans in jail are gay, so I wasn't that surprised. The system was simple: when we used to get opened up in the mornings and after siesta, prisoners get a ten-minute window before the cells were locked again. So in this time the gay couples used to get it on.

GG's cell was two down from me, and one time when I was walking past, I noticed Norris there telling GG to suck his cock. I looked in, and they both saw me. Norris tried to make a joke out of it, saying he wasn't gay and he had a wife. I just turned and walked downstairs to the yard.

GG was due another visit from his family, so the Gitanos and now Norris too were all trying to befriend GG. It was embarrassing how they were putting their arms around him. Norris and the Gitanos were arguing about who had the bigger rights to GG. He had his family visit, and came back in a new sky-blue Adidas tracksuit, with new Nike trainers. He walked onto the yard, and immediately Norris seized him and dragged him into the showers. Everybody knew what was going down. Even the Gitanos took a step back, because they didn't want to fight Norris. The Moroccan took the new tracksuit and trainers and put them on. He gave his shitty old clothes to GG. He then stuck his hand up GG's ass to find the drugs. All he found was some hash, but not the heroin.

Norris came swaggering onto the yard wearing GGs clothes,

with a big smile on his face. He rolled a joint with the hash he had just seized, and he was smoking it openly in the yard (we could do this because the screws didn't care). Manolo and I were talking about what Norris had done.

"I wanna fuck him up," I said.

"Don't get involved, they are all shit," advised Manolo.

GG walked onto the yard. His eyes were puffy like he'd been crying. I walked up to him while everyone was watching. I asked if he was ok, and he told me what happened. GG explained that Norris still believed he had heroin up his ass, and he's waiting for him to shit it out (he confided that he did still have the heroin wrap up his ass). GG was terrified of Norris, and told me that he had been raped him previously.

I told GG to ask the screws to lock him in his cell, and to not go downstairs to socialise. So this is what he did. Norris was fuming that I had become involved. He wanted the heroin badly. Everyone except GG stayed downstairs until it was time for bang up. I could see Norris arguing with the Gitanos. Other junkies were getting involved too. As soon as a screw opened the door to go upstairs to the cells, Norris, the pack of Gitanos and these other desperate junkies all ran up the stairs to GG. Our cells were secured by two doors, one opening into the other. The inner door was just bars and there was a second metal door that closed over them. GG's bars were locked, but the outside door wasn't. When I walked up to the scene, I could see about fifteen heads shouting and swearing. I walked closer and I saw Norris had hold of GG through the bars by his wrist. Norris was spitting on GG repeatedly. I walked up to Norris.

"Let go of him," I warned.

"What's it got to do with you?"

"He owes me money, and I'm getting paid before you," Norris

looked at GG, then to me and he let go of GG's wrist.

"Have him, I'm finished with him," Norris said with a smile.

I told GG to sit on his bed. I then returned to my cell. The screws were coming by that time, so the others dispersed too. Manolo was behind me. Like many old-school lags, he was a homophobic, so didn't want to stick up for GG. However, he didn't like bullying either, so he could see my point.

The next morning, the Gitanos were still hassling GG for smack, but he said he had to pay me. In fact, he had smoked the rest the previous night. I told him to walk the yard with me, and he did. Norris knew I had him under my wing. Maybe he thought I wanted his ass. Then Manolo came up to me, and told GG to go away.

Manolo said, "It don't look good you walking with him. You get to keep your rep up."

Despite this risk to my reputation, I liked talking to GG because he was funny. Now he knew he was safe, he started to open up. GG was only doing a short sentence, and it turned out he was due to go free in a couple of days. I told him jail wasn't for him.

He replied, "I've got no choice but to steal, as nobody will employ a gay Gitano." I could see his point. After his release, I didn't see GG again.

22 JUNGEMENT DAY

Spanish sentencing is all consecutive, unlike England where you can get sentences to run alongside each other, which is called "concurrent". So in Spain if you do six burglaries and get two years for each one, you end up adding them all together and doing a total of twelve years. This is why there were so many people in jail with HIV. They get big sentences, start to share needles, and then many start having sex with each other.

My first and best friend in the wing was Carlo, not to be confused with Carlos the Killer. Apart from both being murderers they couldn't have been more different. Carlo was twenty-six, and was doing twenty-five years for murder. He had been in five-years by the time I met him. He was slightly built and well-educated. This guy wasn't cut out for jail, so he handled it by smoking smack. But he was clean - he didn't inject himself, or fuck anybody. He still thought his girlfriend was going to wait for him, as he thought she owed him.

I felt sorry for my friend. His story went like this. He, and his girlfriend went to a party. They had a good time, and as the night was coming to a close, the only people left were Carlo, his girlfriend and the host. Carlo's girlfriend was fit, so the host had been flirting with her. She had apparently been flirting back. Carlo couldn't handle it as he was insecure, so he started to argue with the host. The host confronted him and told him to leave. Carlo was not a natural fighter, so he panicked and hit his host over the head with a bottle of vodka, cracking his skull and killing him with one shot. This must have been some hit.

Carlo and his girlfriend were shitting it, so they decide to get rid of the body. They wrapped the host up, put him in the boot of Carlo's car, and drove to outback land in the middle of nowhere. They dragged the body out and Carlo decided to burn it, which they did. Then they went home. To nobody's surprise they got caught, and Carlo took all the blame to get his girlfriend off the hook. He got fifteen-years for murder and an extra ten for burning the body. He told me that if he had money, he could have got a decent lawyer to bribe the judges, and he would have received a lesser sentence.

I knew all about this from my previous lawyer who was terrible. My new brief, Antonio Gonzalez, however, was very efficient. He was in his mid-thirties, with short black hair, and he always wore an expensive suit. He looked the business. I told him my story, but it was as if he was hearing and not listening. He already knew what the outcome was going to be.

"I need six thousand pounds to pay the judge and my fees are three thousand," he said.

Antonio was very clear about the sentence I would get. He was high-up in the legal game, and he knew what he was talking about. He received his three-grand from me, and the additional six-grand to bribe my judge with. We had a case for expulsion from the country, so he told me I would get four-and-a-half years in prison. I would have to agree to not enter Spain for ten-years. I also paid for my drug mules Harry and Michelle to get the same treatment, as they didn't have any money themselves. If all went well, they would get the same sentence as me.

The day of sentencing came, and the three of us were taken to court in a van. I remember looking out of the window, and the normal life beyond looked so weird to me. I had only seen bricks and concrete for the past two-years, so it was a shock to see women and families in nice-clothing, walking casually down the street. They looked so soft and happy compared to the hard concrete walls I lived within. I could not imagine being let free into this bright world.

Once we arrived at court, we were bundled out the van into

holding cells, until our slot was up. Then we got taken to the dock. The judge was severe-looking, in his forties with a dark blue suit. There were a few officials sat near him. The courtroom was similar to the ones in England, wooden benches mainly. It was a big case, so the press were there too. Everything was said in formal Spanish. I couldn't make it all out, but I could tell from his manner that my lawyer was quick and efficient in his speech for our defence. I did understand when the judge said, "Cuatro anos y medio" (four and-a-half years). We were ecstatic. It was difficult to hide my joy. In Spain you only do two-thirds of the sentence, and I had done two years already, so I only had one-year left. I could see the end to this nightmare now.

We got took back to prison, and I told the other inmates about my result. You could see who was happy for me, and who wasn't. The Germans weren't happy as they were racist, and they all hoped I would get nine-years. But the Gitanos were happy for me, so they decided to go into the yard and sing and dance for me. One of them had a guitar, and they were singing and flamenco dancing. In prison you got closer to the ones who were leaving, as if a part of you might get to leave with them.

23 THE ARGENTINIAN

Georgio landed on the wing. He was a strong Argentine, in his late thirties, who was doing forty-years for armed robberies and shoot-outs with the Feds. He was six-foot two-inches tall, had long wavy hair, was educated and spoke good English. Georgio was a bank robber in Argentina, and had fled to Spain after killing someone in his home country. Upon his arrival into the country, he carried on robbing in Spain.

He was partnered with two associates for one particular robbery. The gang of three went into the bank, fired a few shots, and demanded money. They got the money, but when they left the bank they were surrounded by armed police. The three robbers had a shootout with the Feds, and Georgio's two friends were shot dead. One cop was also shot dead, and two were injured. Georgio was shot six-times, but didn't die. Instead of calling an ambulance the police took the shot-up Georgio in the van and kicked him to fuck.

When I met Georgio, who was six-years into his sentence by that point, he was still walked with a limp because of the shootings. This bothered him a lot. He was always getting transferred, as he was considered a danger to the authorities. Georgio and I formed a friendship, and I let him sit at my corner table. We trained together, and used to spar. I helped him with his footwork, which made his limp better. He was really pleased about this, and he used to thank me all the time for helping him.

Georgio was very blasé in his manner of explaining things. He would talk about robberies he had done, and how he would just shoot anybody that got in his way. He wasn't impressed with have-a-go heroes. One day while we were sparring, he told me how he was planning an escape. His plan was this: he had a girlfriend on the outside, and she was sorting out a gyrocopter to come and lift him out of the prison yard. Not in this jail, but a jail in Madrid where he was going next. His mate would fly above the jail, shoot the screw in the tower, then drop a rope down for Georgio to grab. He would get lifted out. To me, it all seemed too far-fetched, but I supposed he needed some hope that he would be free someday.

One afternoon Georgio and I were walking the yard. There were four Germans and three Russians also out walking at this time. Lobo was hanging around also. These Germans and Russians only felt safe in numbers. The German, Marcel went up to Lobo and said something to him. Despite being small and physically outmatched by Marcel, Lobo told him to fuck off. Marcel drop kicked him, bringing the little fella crashing to the floor. The whole yard saw this liberty, which it was, as Lobo was only small. So the next moment all the Spanish prisoners, about twelve of them in total, attacked the Germans.

Tensions had been building up because the Germans used to bully everyone else, except their Russian pals. People were getting sick of it. The three Russians came to help the Germans, and there was a mass riot in the yard. It was fuckin' crazy. The screws were holding back from coming out into the yard to end it, as they were fearful of being stabbed, which was a real risk for them.

People were looking at me to join in and help the Spanish, as they knew I had fought previous battles with the Germans.

Georgio turned round to me, and said, "Leave it, Indio. Don't get involved. You're going home in ten-months."

I couldn't risk getting involved in a riot and getting more jailtime, so I just watched. I did feel a bit of a coward for not getting involved, but Georgio was right. I was going home soon. The screw in the tower fired two shots, but nobody stopped fighting. Then about twenty screws burst onto the scene with long bats. They started bashing all the people fighting. Some got bashed, and they weren't even fighting. Order was resumed, and a few prisoners were taken away. Afterwards, I was glad I didn't get involved. The fight lasted only a few moments, and if I'd gotten embroiled in the situation it would have cost me years of my life.

24 THE TOURNAMENT

Thanks to having access to the main gym once a week, my training was coming on well. My maximum bench press was one-hundred and thirty-kilos, about two-hundred and eighty-pounds. On the outside, it used to be one-hundred and ninety-kilos, but I was on steroids then. In prison my body had been clean of steroids for over two-years.

The Germans were taking a steroid called Anapolon. I never found out how they were getting them in, but they had them. I wasn't interested in taking drugs, as my body felt good now I was totally clean. I was at my natural fittest when the gym screw announced that there was going to be a weight lifting competition. It was only going to be the bench press, as that's all there was time for. The competition was scheduled to be held in two weeks' time. There were three weight categories: light, middle and heavy. All four modulos of the prison were included. Everyone who trained was excited, as this was the first time something like this had happened in the history of Fontcalent.

The Germans were confident, especially Marcel. He was full of steroids now. The arrogant lag had ballooned up in weight, yet was only benching about the same as me. We were all training hard in preparation. Lobo entered his name for the lightweight, two Gitanos entered their names for the middleweight class.

These two Gitanos were Pirata and Savvy. They both had HIV and were similar stamp: skinny with long greasy hair. They never used to train. The reason for joining in was just so they could get off Modulo 4 and try and score drugs off people from different wings. Georgio, two Germans, Marcel, Frank, and myself were all in the heavyweight class.

The day of the competition came, and it worked like this:

there was maximum of ten people from each wing, and we had four wings in total. The weight on the bar started at sixty-kilos (just over one-hundred and thirty-pounds).

To save time, everybody took a turn, and had to clear the weight for one rep. I used these early weights to warm up, so I repped out a few, and so did the others. The weight was going up ten kilos after each round, so we soon reached one-hundred kilos.

The lightweights were dropping out, and I think Lobo came last. The lightweight winner was some Algerian from Modulo 1. By-the-time the weight went up to one hundred and-ten kilos, the middleweights had also dropped out. The middleweight winner was some Spanish kid from Modulo 3. Georgio had also dropped out by now, and there were only four of us left: me, Marcel, Frank and some Spanish kid from Modulo 1. The weight by then was one hundred and twenty kilos and Marcel cleared it. Frank went next and failed. The Spanish kid cleared it too. I went and cleared it easy. I was feeling strong.

The weight was increased to one hundred and thirty kilos. Marcel went up and he did it, but it wasn't the cleanest of presses. The Spanish kid failed, which wasn't a surprise, as he had struggled with the previous rep. This was my maximum weight I had completed since I was clean off steroids, but I was confident and I did it.

The weight was now at one hundred and forty kilos. I had never done this weight before. I hadn't seen Marcel do it either, but he was full of steroids, and I knew what power they can give you. Marcel stepped up. The other Germans were bigging him up, and he was walking about with his chest sticking out. He got hold of the bar and brought it down slowly, not a good technique as it saps your energy. He pushed it up, but his left arm was lagging, and his right was up. He was struggling, but carried on until he shook and folded. He was devastated. You could see the anger in his face. Marcel was bright red and looked as if he was going to burst.

It was my turn and I knew had to do this. There was too much pride on the line. Marcel and I were enemies, but we had never physically fought each other. He was desperate to beat me. Georgio and Lobo pumped me up, and were telling me that I had to do this. otherwise I would draw with the German. Everybody was tense. We all knew this was a lot more than a weightlifting competition.

I stepped up and I was feeling good. I got a hold of the bar. People were shouting, giving me encouragement. I lifted it off, and dropped it quickly to save energy. Then I pressed it. The weight was feeling heavy as fuck, but I went through the gears, first, second, third.

People were shouting, "Vamos!" (come on).

I let out a scream, and I cleared it.

I jumped off the bench and shouted, "Fuck yeah!"

Georgio and Lobo came over and gave me high fives. I felt brilliant, then I looked over at Marcel. He walked over to me, and shook my hand. The other Germans didn't. We all got taken back to the wing, and everyone back there was waiting for the result. They had all wanted to go, but they weren't permitted. I burst through the doors to the yard, and I just my right hand in the air, just like my footballing hero Alan Shearer. The other inmates went wild cheering me on.

I had a cassette player, which I had taken off somebody for not paying their debt. I used to use it to record songs from the radio. This is how I got my entertainment. There was a good radio station we could receive from Benidorm, and I recorded some good songs from there. One song was the New Order England football song, the one with the rap by legendary England player John Barnes. The European championship was on, and the

Spanish love football, even more than the English. In particular, they hated the England team in Spain, and probably still do.

An England match was on. The television was in the hall area, and it was a small screen encased in metal with a plastic clear front. We were all watching the match and everybody wanted the opposing team to win, as they all hated England so much. I was the only England supporter. I don't remember the exact result, but we won. Everyone was devastated, and I was laughing my head off, but they were taking it quite seriously. We went for our dinner, then we were locked up for the afternoon siesta. Normally people go to sleep for a couple of hours, but I was buzzing off the England win and I couldn't sleep. So I decided to put my tunes on, and the England song by New Order came up. Now I was excited, so I got my radio and put it on the bars on my window and turned it up full blast. It was silent outside before, but with the high walls in the yard the sound was bouncing off making the song really loud. Next thing the whole wing was shouting abuse at me and telling me to turn it off, but I didn't. I let the song finish to the end.

25 LIBERTAD

By this time, I was really looking forward to going back to England. I'd had my fill of the place now. I also suspected that I had HIV, because I had had so many fights with people who had the disease and I had spilled their blood on me. I eventually did get tested, and to my relief the results were negative. I couldn't believe it, so I went back and got another one to make sure. That was negative too.

It was morning time, and Georgio and I were in the gym. A screw came in and called my name out. He said, I had to go to the office. I went over and the Chief Screw (Jefe or "boss" in Spanish) came to the window. He was a thickset man in his mid-thirties, standing six-foot three-inches. The boss was always ok with me, or better than the rest anyway. For example, my cell used to be covered in pictures of topless girls, and when other screws searched it they would angrily rip most of the photos down. But when Jefe used to come to search my cell, he would just smile at my pictures.

"Sandhu you are going home," said Jefe as I stood to attention in his office. He showed me some papers.

I saw, I had got an immediate expulsion, despite having six-months of my sentence left to serve. Previously, all my lawyer Antonio had promised was that he would try to get me booted out the country instead of finishing my sentence. He warned it would be difficult, because of the amount of drugs was arrested with. I couldn't believe that he had pulled it off. To me he was the best lawyer in the world.

Jefe told me to pack my things, and a van would come for me and take me to the airport. I was leaving in half-an-hour. I walked into the yard and screamed out, "Libertad!" (Freedom). Georgio, Lobo, the Gitanos, and my other friends all came to me. Everyone was hugging and kissing me. It was the best feeling in the world.

A screw took me to my cell, and let me pack my things. I had a fair amount of stuff, so I packed everything up. I had lots of books and magazines, clothes which I had bought in jail, and lots of other shit like Walkmans, which I had confiscated off people to pay their debts.

I took everything downstairs to the hall, and waiting for me there were all the scavengers eagerly anticipating what I was going to give them. I told them all to fuck off. I gave my best things to my friends, and my clothes to the Gitanos. The only things I left jail with were my letters, some money I had made, and a lump of hash shoved up my ass. I wasn't going to leave that behind.

I said goodbye to them all, Carlos, Lobo and Georgio were all still in Modulo 4, and they were genuinely happy for me. The Germans couldn't believe what was going on, so Artur the older one came up to me.

He said, "How are you going home early?"

"I've got expulsion," I replied.

I explained how instead of sending you to prison, the courts can expel you from their country for a certain amount of years. I got expelled for ten-years. I knew this gave the Germans a hope too, as they were looking at ten-years behind bars. I said goodbye to them, and wished them luck. Despite the aggravation I had with the Germans in the past, I was so buzzing in that moment that there were no hard feelings left. I was so happy, I would have said goodbye to serial killer Fred West if he had been there. I was taken to the van, and Harry and Michelle were there too. We couldn't hug each other because we were handcuffed at the back, but we all had a massive smile on our faces.

We were taken to Alicante airport, and placed in holding cells in a basement. The three-of-us were all talking at the same time, in particular about what we were going to do first when we get home. We were held there for about two-hours, when two Feds came down and unlocked us. I was just wearing what I had on in the gym, which was shorts and a vest. I was so excited, I had forgotten to change, and I had just given all my clothes away to the Gitanos.

We were re-handcuffed to the front, and taken onto the

plane by the back entrance, seated at the back. The two Feds were there too, on either side of us. We had a decent flight, we weren't allowed to get up, and the other passengers were kept well-away from us.

We landed in Gatwick with no baggage, as the Spanish police had taken it all previously. We were taken straight to immigration, and cleared.

Then the Spanish Feds unlocked us and said, "Ok, you're free to go."

We walked out into the duty free section, and I changed my pesetas into pounds. I then went and bought a packet of Walkers cheese and onion crisps, and went and sat on the grass outside. I hadn't seen grass or crisps in quite a while. Eating the crisps on the grass felt so fucking good.

That day and the whole night, we just walked around London, taking everything in. It all looked so awesome. Then we got the coach back to Newcastle at seven AM. I was only out for just over a year, when I got another seven stretch. This time it was for conspiracy to supply class A drugs, blackmail and controlling prostitution.

23362075R00054

Printed in Great Britain
by Amazon